DOCTORAL DISSERTATIONS IN MUSICOLOGY

DOCTORAL DISSERTATIONS

IN

MUSICOLOGY

THIRD EDITION

Compiled by

HELEN HEWITT

AMERICAN MUSICOLOGICAL SOCIETY

Philadelphia, 1961

Joint Committee of the Music Teachers National Association and the American Musicological Soc[...] (handwritten)

First edition, Copyright, 1952, by
THE MUSIC TEACHERS NATIONAL ASSOCIATION, INC.

Second edition, Copyright, 1957, by
THE MUSIC TEACHERS NATIONAL ASSOCIATION, INC.

Third edition, Copyright, 1961, by
THE AMERICAN MUSICOLOGICAL SOCIETY

———

Music

gift of Prob's [...] (handwritten)

ML
128
M8
J74
1961
c.2

THIRD EDITION

B834674 (handwritten)
Ex 553/G (handwritten)

Available from
THE AMERICAN MUSICOLOGICAL SOCIETY
204 Hare Building, Philadelphia 4, Pa.
$2.50 per copy, postpaid

Table of Contents

Foreword

THE YEAR 1961 marks the tenth anniversary of the list of *Doctoral Dissertations in Musicology*. By 1950 enough activity had already taken place in musicological research in the United States so that a need was felt for a record of the many doctoral dissertations which were already on library shelves of universities from Massachusetts to California. The idea for such a listing was brought forward at a joint meeting of the Music Teachers National Association and the American Musicological Society in December of 1950.

During the past ten years the two societies have worked together harmoniously in the annual listing of dissertations completed during the year, as well as in making known subjects selected for investigation during the same period.

Over the past few years, however, the feeling has grown that the material reported was of more professional interest to the members of the American Musicological Society, and that it was primarily the province of this society to assume continuance of the project. It is, therefore, as a result of mutual agreement among the officers of the two societies that the publication will continue henceforth under the sole auspices of the American Musicological Society. In retrospect, we wish to express our gratitude to the Music Teachers National Association: their generous co-operation and support have made possible the realization of a project whose usefulness for musicological studies has by now been amply demonstrated.

Cornell University   DONALD J. GROUT

Ithaca, N. Y.
April 18, 1961

Preface to the First Edition

DURING THE PAST twenty-five years a growing interest has been shown by the American student of music in that branch of his profession dealing with research: i.e., musicology. Of late it has become increasingly felt that advanced studies related to musicology should be brought together in such a manner as to make possible a survey of what has been done and is being done in musicology and related fields. While the present list is not the first to attempt to satisfy such a need, it is perhaps the first to take into account studies which are in progress at American institutions as well as those already completed. For reasons of space only dissertations written for the doctor's degree are included.

The present project was begun under the auspices of the Committee on Musicology of the Music Teachers National Association of which Louise Cuyler is chairman. The subject was discussed at the annual convention held in Washington, D. C., during December, 1950, in a meeting of the Musicology Section of the MTNA. Since the American Musicological Society was also convening at the same time and place, it was decided that the two societies would co-operate in planning and carrying out this project. The committee having had charge of the compilation of this list of Doctoral Dissertations in Musicology and Related Fields is, therefore, a joint committee of MTNA and AMS.

The committee has taken advantage of such information as has already appeared in print. From 1912 to 1938 the Library of Congress published a *List of American Doctoral Dissertations Printed in 19—*, Washington, D. C. Although this appeared annually during this period, it listed only those dissertations which were published. A still more useful source of information, since it included unpublished dissertations as well, was *Doctoral Dissertations Accepted by American Universities 19— - 19—* compiled for the National Research Council and the American Council of Learned Societies by the Association of Research Libraries. (New York, H. W. Wilson Co.) This also was published annually, beginning with the year 1933-1934, under the editorship of Donald B. Goodchild and is still appearing.

The American Council of Learned Societies has continued to show its interest in musicology through its support of four other projects, each of which contributed further items. The first of these was the survey made by W. Oliver Strunk entitled *State and Resources of Musicology in the United States*. This was issued as American Council of Learned Societies *Bulletin No. 19* in December, 1932. On pp. 43-51 Strunk gives a list of studies in musicology made in connection with both master's and doctor's degrees. Following this came *A Report on Publication and Research in*

Musicology and Allied Fields in the United States 1932-38, compiled for the Committee on Musicology of the American Council of Learned Societies, Washington, D. C., 1938. This was compiled by D. H. Daugherty and was issued in mimeographed form. This also contained a list of theses. In 1940 appeared *A Bibliography of Periodical Literature in Musicology and Allied Fields and a Record of Graduate Theses Accepted. No. 1: October 1, 1938-September 30, 1939*, assembled for the Committee on Musicology of the American Council of Learned Societies by D. H. Daugherty. This contained on pp. 126-135 a list of "Graduate Theses Accepted" between the dates given in the title, and again included both master's and doctor's theses. This was followed in 1943 by a companion *Bibliography of Periodical Literature . . . No. 2: October 1, 1939-September 30, 1940*, assembled for the Committee on Musicology of the American Council of Learned Societies by D. H. Daugherty, Leonard Ellinwood, and Richard S. Hill. This, however, contained no list of graduate theses.

At the request of the Committee on Musicology of the American Council of Learned Societies, Catharine Keyes Miller prepared a "List of Graduate Theses in Musicology and Allied Fields Accepted by Educational Institutions in the United States October 1, 1939-September 30, 1946." This list began where Daugherty's list left off, but has not as yet been brought up to 1952. Through the courtesy of Charles Seeger, chairman of the Committee on Musicology of the ACLS, Mrs. Miller's list was placed at the disposal of the present committee. It was thought at first that all the titles assembled by Mrs. Miller might find a place in the present compilation. However, when the decision was reached to limit the present study to doctoral dissertations, only about a tenth of Mrs. Miller's titles fell into this category, the remainder representing work done for the master's degree. Our hearty thanks are due the American Council of Learned Societies, however, for their consent to our use of this portion of Mrs. Miller's typescript.

One other list including both master's and doctor's theses should also be mentioned here. That is the *Bibliography of Research Studies in Music Education 1932-1944* prepared by the Committee on Research in Music Education of the Music Educators National Conference, edited by Arnold M. Small, and published in 1944. A number of doctoral dissertations entered there will also be found in the present list. Since the MENC bibliography expressly accepted "only those studies which by their titles indicated a contribution to the *teaching of music*," it has seemed unnecessary to include all such theses here, and the present list has taken from this source only those which seemed to be closely related to musicology.

A fairly large number of items appear in the present list which will not be found in any of the sources just mentioned. These have been contributed by both scholars and librarians from institutions throughout the

10

country. To obtain titles of dissertations in progress, institutions were circularized in the fall of 1951. The response was most gratifying, for replies brought not only indications of studies in progress, but, in some cases, full lists of completed dissertations as well. The present list cannot claim to be exhaustive as far as either category is concerned, but it is fairly representative of musicological activity at the doctoral level in the American university today. The many contributors who have made it so are too numerous to name, but the committee wishes to express its heartfelt thanks to them for their work.

It should be pointed out that the distinguishing feature of the present compilation is the inclusion of dissertations in progress. The value of this feature is dependent upon its being kept up to date. It is hoped that this list can be revised and reissued annually. The committee therefore urgently requests that omissions and corrections be sent to the chairman as promptly as possible.

Our acknowledgments are due to the American Musicological Society for the interest it has shown in this work from its inception, and we are particularly indebted to the Music Teachers National Association which has contributed the necessary financial support.

HANS THEODORE DAVID, *University of Michigan*
LLOYD HIBBERD, *North Texas State College*
JAN LARUE, *Wellesley College*
CATHARINE KEYES MILLER, *New York Public Library*
CLEMENT MILLER, *Cleveland Institute of Music*
HANS NATHAN, *Michigan State College*
HELEN HEWITT, *North Texas State College, Chairman*

North Texas State College
February 20, 1952

Preface to the Second Edition

At the close of the Preface to the First (1952) Edition of this list of *Doctoral Dissertations in Musicology*, the hope was expressed that the list might be kept up to date from year to year. This hope has been fulfilled, not by expanding the entire *List* each year, but by publishing "Supplements" annually. These Supplements would not have been possible had it not been for the faithful reporting of the needed information by one individual at each of the educational institutions involved, and the collaboration of the editors of the periodicals published by the two organizations sponsoring this project. These Supplements have appeared both in the *American Music Teacher*[1] and in the *Journal of the American Musicological Society*.[2]

Since the original *List* of 1952 is now out of print, and the task of consulting so many Supplements is becoming increasingly difficult, the two societies have determined to issue a new edition.

During the intervening period of five years certain suggestions have been made as to ways in which the *List* might achieve greater usefulness. As a result of these suggestions, this second edition has been so altered as to bear little resemblance to the first.

The spirit that prompted the selection of the 482 items of the first edition was that of helpfulness. To this end some 237 items were included which were written outside departments of music, but which touched on musical matters to a greater or less degree. Since these were included there, they can still easily be referred to, but they have been removed from this second edition, leaving more space for topics undertaken since 1952, and permitting this second edition to present a more unified musicological front.

Of the 550 items of the second edition, 231 have been carried over from the first edition. Of these, 132 were already completed in 1952. Of the 99 which were in progress in 1952, 70 have reached completion; the 29 others are still in progress.[3] In the present list of 550 topics, 342 are completed dissertations; 208 are reported in progress. While only 132

---

[1] "First Supplement to *Doctoral Dissertations in Musicology*," *American Music Teacher*, II.5 (May-June, 1953), 10, 16-17. "Second Supplement . . . ," *AMT*, III.5 (May-June, 1954), 8-9, 16. "Third Supplement . . . ," *AMT*, IV.5 (May-June, 1955), 8-9, 20. "Fourth Supplement . . . ," *AMT*, V.5 (May-June, 1956), 6-7, 15.

[2] "Supplement (1953-1954) to *Doctoral Dissertations in Musicology*," *Journal of the American Musicological Society*, VII (1954), 131-140. "Supplement (1955) . . . ," *JAMS*, VIII (1955), 116-122. "Supplement (1956) . . . ," *JAMS*, IX (1956), 202-209.

[3] Fourteen other topics, not counted in these figures, have been abandoned, or were reported without authorization, or, because of some other error, have not been included in the new edition.

musicological dissertations had been completed by 1952, 212 more have been completed within the last five years; there are, in fact, more (208) in progress today than had been completed (132) up to 1952; almost as many, in fact, as the combined total (231) of both completed and uncompleted dissertations in 1952.

The list of 550 topics, completed or still in progress, found in the present *List*, represents the work for the doctorate in music done in this country[4] from 1905, the year in which the first Ph.D. in music was granted by an American university[5], through June, 1957.

On the whole, those reporting dissertation topics have been of a single mind as to the interpretation of the word "musicology." It has meant "research in the history of music." At Yale University the degree is named "Ph.D. in History of Music." Other institutions call it merely "Ph.D. in Music." A few universities offer more than one degree in the field of music: "Ph.D. in Musicology," "Ph.D. in Theory," or "Ph.D. in Composition." Dissertations written for the degree in Theory have been included here so far as they deal with the theoretical aspects of composition that would be of interest to the musicologist. Topics dealing with the "psychology of music" have been considered as more properly belonging to the field of psychology than to that of music; those dealing with acoustics or physics have been omitted for a similar reason. Most of the dissertations written for degrees in "Music Education" have been considered more properly "education" than "music." However, the situation exists in which one or more musicologists hold positions on a faculty where no doctoral degree is yet offered in the field of "musicology." In such situations a dissertation may be accepted for a degree in "Theory" or "Music Education" which is more correctly classified as "Musicology." A few of these topics have been included and amount to perhaps 20 out of the 550 items.

From the very inception of this project certain other omissions were considered advisable. For a number of reasons theses written for the master's degree were not to be included; musical works written for the "Ph.D. in Composition" were also, by common consent, to be omitted, because the basic purpose of the *List* was not to give a full report on all degrees awarded in the field of music, but to record progress in musical research at the doctoral level, in order to enable faculty and students at one institution to know what was being done elsewhere.

Quite recently a new, and I believe experimental, degree is being offered at some institutions. This is known as the "Doctor of Musical Arts" degree and is awarded primarily for excellence in performance, but with an attendant requirement of a piece of research. Although research papers

[4] One Canadian dissertation has been included; see No. 161.
[5] Harvard University; see No. 469.

14

written for this degree are not included in the present edition, one piece of work has been brought to my attention which is of such calibre as to have warranted inclusion. This is Hans Lampl's 400-page annotated translation of the *Syntagma Musicum III* of Michael Praetorius done for the D.M.A. in Conducting at the University of Southern California (1957).

Another important change in the present edition is that made in the organization of the topics. This change was brought about by a suggestion that a grouping of the topics according to historical periods would be more useful than the arrangement employed in the first edition, where quite unrelated topics stood side by side because they had been dealt with at the same university. This new method of arrangement has been tried in the present edition, but the task of classification has proved a difficult one. Too many titles left one uncertain as to their proper category, some even requiring consultation of reference books such as Eitner, so little known was the individual in question that neither Grove's *Dictionary* nor the Norton series of histories made mention of him.

Uncertainty as to correct classification might have been avoided had it been possible to organize the topics by historical periods alone, but a few topical classifications proved to be necessary. In the early part of May each institution was sent a list of its dissertations, compiled from the original *List* and the various Supplements, together with a proposed classification for each topic and a request that each be either confirmed or corrected. In most instances the new classification according to period was approved by the representative of the institution. In some instances, especially in the field of "Theory," topics have been placed under that heading by request. It is my hope, however, that with the help of the extensive Index items dealing with any subject matter may be located without undue difficulty.

Another important change in the organization has been that the "dissertations in progress" have not been placed in isolation at the end, but have been incorporated in the body of the list. Within each classification the institutions having dissertations within that field are listed in alphabetical order; within the institution the completed dissertations are listed first in the alphabetical order of their authors; then follow similarly the dissertations in progress. As in the first edition, the asterisk (*) has been used to identify dissertations in progress.

I should like here to thank most sincerely all those who have devoted both valuable time and careful attention to my periodic requests. The ultimate success of this project will be due to their continuing co-operation; its completeness and accuracy will reflect the effort they expend and the care they bestow upon it.

My gratitude also goes out to all those who, even unwittingly, by some casual comment, have contributed to improvements in this list; more particularly, however, to Dr. Michael Winesanker of Texas Christian University and Dr. Paul Pisk of the University of Texas for their participation in a panel discussion on "Doctoral Dissertation Listings" at a meeting of the Texas Chapter of the American Musicological Society held in Waco, Texas, in the spring of 1957.

I should also like to thank my colleague at North Texas State College, Dr. Lloyd Hibberd, to whom I have turned for all sorts of help; and four of my graduate students, Mac Jones, William McKee, Kenton Parton, and Phillip Sims, each of whom volunteered to help in any way that he could—with typing, indexing, or final checking. Every form of assistance was most welcome and gratefully accepted during the Texas heat of June and July, 1957.

In conclusion may I express my appreciation of the fine support given this project by Dr. J. Murray Barbour, President of the American Musicological Society, and Dr. Duane H. Haskell, President of the Music Teachers National Association. With their full co-operation, this second edition has been a joint project of the two societies, in which each has had an equal share. The project was initiated in 1950 within the Standing Committee on Musicology of MTNA, and the present Chairman of that committee, Dr. Robert A. Warner, has lent his full support to this new edition. A special debt of gratitude is due Dr. Gustave Reese, representing AMS, and Mr. S. Turner Jones, representing MTNA, who have been entrusted with the actual publication and distribution of this compilation.

HELEN HEWITT
School of Music
North Texas State College

Denton, Texas
July 20, 1957

Preface to the Third Edition

W ITH THIS Third Edition the list of *Doctoral Dissertations in Musicology* reaches another milestone. Since the preparation of material for the Second Edition, two Supplements have appeared in the *Journal of the American Musicological Society*.[1] Despite the passage of only four years, the number of entries has increased from 550 in the Second Edition to 829 in this Third Edition.

Since the arrangement of the items follows the scheme established in the Second Edition, there is no need for comment on this aspect, but since the microfilming of theses and dissertations has increased, and the "publication" of such studies in the form of microcards has become more frequent, some explanation of the method employed in recording information concerning such reproductions seems desirable.

All of the microfilming has been done by University Microfilms, Inc., Ann Arbor, Michigan, and orders for films may be placed directly with this firm. Abstracts of dissertations they have filmed may be read in the volumes which they issue monthly and which are entitled *Dissertation Abstracts.* . . . At the beginning of their enterprise they gave their production number for each film; of late they have given the library-card number assigned the film by the Library of Congress. In the following pages, then, the reference "UM 2346," for example, denotes the production number 2346 of University Microfilms, Inc. The symbol "LC No.: Mic 60-2346," on the other hand, indicates that the Library of Congress has assigned "Mic 60-2346" as the call number for the film of the dissertation in question.

Although microcards are made by various firms, all the dissertations in music seem to have been produced by the University of Rochester Press. I have therefore used the symbol "UR" to indicate that a dissertation may be procured on a microcard. In so doing, I have followed Miss Eva Maude Tilton, who has compiled a catalogue of all microcards published through December, 1958. Her book is entitled *A Union List of Publications in Opaque Microforms* (New York: The Scarecrow Press, 1959). The entries in her catalogue are numbered consecutively; the number I have given following the symbol "UR" is that assigned the item in her catalogue. Any dissertation followed by such a symbol ("UR 2346," for example) may be ordered from the University of Rochester Press, Rush Rhees Library, River Campus Station, Rochester 20, New York. Inclusion of Miss Tilton's number would serve only to confirm the title.

---

[1] "Supplement (1958-59) to *Doctoral Dissertations in Musicology*," *JAMS*, XI (1958), 217-226; "Supplement (1960) . . . ," *JAMS*, XII (1959), 215-224.

Once again I should like to thank all those persons—one at each university—who have so faithfully reported to me each year information which now appears in the ensuing pages. But for their continued loyal co-operation this listing would have little value. Most particularly I should like to thank Mr. Kenton Parton, a doctoral candidate at North Texas State College, for the generous contribution of his time and talents in compiling the Index of Subjects. His services, freely offered and most gratefully accepted, saved me many hours of detailed work. I should also like to add a personal word of acknowledgement of the friendly association I have had during the past ten years with Mr. S. Turner Jones, editor of the *American Music Teacher*, and Dr. Charles Warren Fox, editor of *JAMS*, both of whom always managed to find a place for the Supplements in their periodicals. Finally, to Professor David G. Hughes, for his willingness to assume responsibility for the publication of this Third Edition in addition to his already heavy duties as Editor-in-Chief of *JAMS*—my deepest and most sincere gratitude.

North Texas State College   HELEN HEWITT
Denton, Texas
April 1, 1961

Institutions Awarding Doctoral Degrees
in Musicology

(Ph.D.: Music, Musicology, History of Music)

in the United States of America

Symbol	Institution	Location
Bos	Boston University	Boston, Mass.
Brand	Brandeis University	Waltham, Mass.
Cal B	University of California at Berkeley	Berkeley, Calif.
Cal LA	University of California at Los Angeles	Los Angeles, Calif.
Cath	Catholic University of America	Washington, D. C.
Chi	University of Chicago	Chicago, Ill.
Colum	Columbia University	New York, N. Y.
Cor	Cornell University	Ithaca, N. Y.
Harv	Harvard University	Cambridge, Mass.
Ill	University of Illinois	Urbana, Ill.
Ind	Indiana University	Bloomington, Ind.
Iowa	State University of Iowa	Iowa City, Iowa
Mich	University of Michigan	Ann Arbor, Mich.
Minn	University of Minnesota	Minneapolis, Minn.
N Car	University of North Carolina	Chapel Hill, N. Car.
N Tex	North Texas State College	Denton, Texas
N Wes	Northwestern University	Evanston, Ill.
NY Gr	New York University, Graduate School of Arts and Science	New York, N. Y.
Peab	George Peabody College for Teachers	Nashville, Tenn.
Penn	University of Pennsylvania	Philadelphia, Pa.
Prin	Princeton University	Princeton, N. J.
Rad	Radcliffe College	Cambridge, Mass.
Roch	University of Rochester, Eastman School of Music	Rochester, N. Y.
S Cal	University of Southern California	Los Angeles, Calif.
Stan	Stanford University	Stanford, Calif.
Tex	University of Texas	Austin, Texas
Wash	University of Washington	Seattle, Wash.
Wash StL	Washington University	St. Louis, Mo.
Wis	University of Wisconsin	Madison, Wis.
W Res	Western Reserve University	Cleveland, Ohio
Yale	Yale University	New Haven, Conn.

Institutions Awarding Other Doctoral Degrees in Music

(Ph.D.: Theory, Music Theory, Music Education;
Ed.D.: Music Education; D.S.M.)

Flor	Florida State University, School of Music	Tallahassee, Fla.
Mich St	Michigan State University	East Lansing, Mich.
NY Ed	New York University, School of Education	New York, N. Y.
Ohio	Ohio State University	Columbus, Ohio
U Theol	Union Theological Seminary, School of Sacred Music	New York, N. Y.

Institutions Which Have Awarded the Ph.D. Degree in Music by Exception and Only Once

Clare	Claremont Graduate School	Claremont, Calif.
Tor	University of Toronto	Toronto, Ont. (Canada)

DOCTORAL DISSERTATIONS IN MUSICOLOGY

ANTIQUITY
(— *ca.* 300)

S Cal

1. Turrell, Frances Berry, "Modulation: A Study of Its Pre-History from Aristoxenus to Henry Glarean." 800 pp. (Ph.D., Musicology, 1956)
   UR 2891.

MIDDLE AGES
(*ca.* 300-1400)

Brand

2. *Ponte, Joseph P., III, "The *Musica disciplina* of Aurelianus Reomensis."

Cal LA

3. Marrocco, W. Thomas, "Jacopo da Bologna and His Works." 108 pp., text; 116 pp., music. (Ph.D., Music, 1952)
   Published as *The Music of Jacopo da Bologna*. Berkeley and Los Angeles, The University of California Press, 1954. *University of California Publications in Music, Vol. V*. xi, 162 pp.

Cath

4. *McShane, Margaret, "The Music of the Mediaeval Drama."

Colum

5. *Sanders, Ernest, "*Cantus-firmus* Treatment in the English Mediaeval Repertoire."
6. *Weakland, *Rev.* Rembert, "The Antiphon of the Ambrosian Chant."

Cor

7. Andrews, Frederick Sturges, "Mediaeval Modal Theory." 210 pp. (Ph.D., Musicology, 1935)
8. Bush, Helen Evelyn, "The Emergence of the Chordal Concept in the Polyphonic Period." 265 pp. (Ph.D., Musicology, 1939)
   Abstract in *Abstracts of Theses* (Cornell University, 1939)

23

Harv

9. Hughes, David Grattan, "A View of the Passing of Gothic Music: Line and Counterpoint, 1380-1430." xxiii, 271 pp. (Ph.D., Music, 1956)

10. Layton, Billy Jim, "Italian Music for the Ordinary of the Mass, 1300-1450." x, 415 pp. (Ph.D., Music, 1960)

11. Spiess, Lincoln B., "Polyphony in Theory and Practice from the 9th Century to the Close of the 13th Century." 3 vols. in 5: Vol. I, 206 pp., text; Vol. II, 156 pp., text; Vol. III, 270 pp. in 3 parts, music. (Ph.D., Music, 1948)

12. Velimirović, Miloš Milorad, "The Byzantine Elements in Early Slavic Chant." 2 vols.: Vol. I, 396 pp., text; Vol. II, cxxv, 64 pp., appendices and plates. (Ph.D., Music, 1957)

Ind

13. Jesson, Roy Hart, "Ambrosian Chant: The Music of the Mass." 178 pp. (Ph.D., Musicology, 1955)
    UM 12,833. DA XV.8, 1411.

14. Johnson, Mildred Jane, "The 37 Motets of the *Codex Ivrea*." 459 pp. in 2 vols.: Vol. I, commentary; Vol. II, transcriptions. (Ph.D., Musicology, 1955)
    UM 13,053. DA XV.9, 1627.

15. White, John Reeves, "Music of the Early Italian *Ars Nova* (*ca.* 1325-1375)." 554 pp. in 2 vols. (Ph.D., Musicology, 1952)

16. *Burris, Jane Gaddis, "A Study of the Two-Part *Clausulae* of the Florentine Codex (Biblioteca Medicea-Laurenziana: *Pluteus 29:1*)." (Musicology)

17. *Colton, Donald, "The *Conducti* of MS Madrid 20486." (Musicology)

18. *Morgan, Glen, "Stylistic Features of the Music of Machaut." (Theory)

19. *Yates, Hadley, "A History of the Cadence in Polyphonic Music to 1500." (Theory)

Iowa

20. Crane, Frederick Baron, "A Study of Theoretical Writings on Musical Form to *ca.* 1460." 319 pp. (Ph.D., Musicology, 1960)
    LC No.: Mic 60-5645. DA XXI.7, 1962.

NY Gr

21. Karp, Theodore, "The Works of the Châtelain de Coucy: An

Analytical Study." 2 vols.: Vol. I, 384 pp., commentary; Vol. II, 197 pp., transcriptions. (Ph.D., Music, 1960)

22. Thurston, Ethel, "The *Conductus* Compositions in Manuscript Wolfenbüttel 1206." 2 vols.: Vol. I, 231 pp., commentary; Vol. II, 311 pp., transcriptions. (Ph.D., Music, 1954)
LC No.: Mic 58-4999. DA XVIII.6, 2162.

NY Ed

23. Burne, *Rev.* Martin Joseph, "Mass Cycles in Early Graduals: A Study of the Ordinary of the Mass Cycles Found in Mediaeval and Renaissance Graduals in Libraries in the United States." 237 pp. (Ph.D., Music Education, 1956)
UM 17,638. DA XVI.10, 1915.

Penn

24. Flindell, Edwin Frederick, III, "The Achievements of the Notre Dame School." 464 pp. (Ph.D., Theory, 1959)
LC No.: Mic 59-4614. DA XX.6, 2323.

Prin

25. *Evans, Paul R., "The St. Martial Tropes."
26. *MacDonald, Royal B., "An Italian Gradual of the Eleventh Century in the Walters Gallery, Baltimore."
27. *Thomas, Isaac, "An Early Stage of the Paleo-Byzantine Notation."
28. *Treitler, Leo, "Origins of the *Conductus*."

Roch

29. Ellinwood, Leonard Webster, "The Works of Francesco Landini." 2 vols.: Vol. I, 87 pp., commentary; Vol. II, 154 pp., musical examples and transcriptions. (Ph.D., Musicology, 1936)
Published as *The Works of Francesco Landini*, ed. Leonard Ellinwood. Cambridge, Mass., The Mediaeval Academy of America, 1939. *The Mediaeval Academy of America Publication No. 36, Studies and Documents, No. 3.* 316 pp.

30. Haban, *Sister* M. Teresine, "The Hymnody of the Roman Catholic Church: Historical Survey with an Analysis of Musical Styles." 471 pp. (Ph.D., Theory, 1956)
UR 2797.

31. Hannas, Ruth, "The Evolution of Harmonic Consciousness: A Study of Pre-Eighteenth-Century Technics." 420 pp. (Ph.D., Musicology, 1934)

S Cal

32. Marquis, George W., "Contrapuntal and Harmonic Tendencies in Fourteenth-Century France." 705 pp. (Ph.D., Music, 1950)
    UR 1931.

Stan

33. *Harrison, Gregory A., "The Monophonic Music in the *Roman de Fauvel.*"

U Theol

34. Allinger, Helen, "The Mozarabic Hymnal and Chant with Special Emphasis on the Hymns of Prudentius." 233 pp. (D.S.M. 1953)

Yale

35. Carpenter, Nan Cooke, "Music in the Mediaeval and Renaissance Universities." 581 pp. in 2 vols. (Ph.D., History of Music, 1948)
    Published under the same title. Norman, The University of Oklahoma Press, 1958. xiii, 394 pp.
36. Crocker, Richard Lincoln, "The Repertoire of Proses at Saint Martial de Limoges (Tenth and Eleventh Centuries)." 546 pp. in 2 vols. (Ph.D., History of Music, 1957)
37. Seay, Albert, "The *Declaratio Musicae Disciplinae* of Ugolino of Orvieto." Critical introduction and text, 1220 pp. (Ph.D., History of Music, 1954)
38. Tischler, Hans, "The Motet in Thirteenth-Century France." 552 pp. in 2 vols. (Ph.D., History of Music, 1942)
39. Waite, William Gilman, "The Rhythm of the Twelfth-Century *Organum* in France." 3 vols. (Ph.D., History of Music, 1951)
    The text and about one-third of the transcriptions published as *The Rhythm of Twelfth-Century Polyphony: Its Theory and Practice* by William G. Waite. New Haven, Yale University Press, 1954. *Yale Studies in the History of Music, Vol. II.* 141 pp., introduction; 245 pp., transcription of Leonin's *Magnus Liber Organi de Gradali et Antiphonario* after MS Wolfenbüttel 677, *olim* Helmstadt 628.
40. Williams, (Mrs.) Sarah Jane, "The Music of Guillaume de Machaut." 396 pp. (Ph.D., History of Music, 1952)
41. *Gushee, Lawrence, "The *Musica disciplina* of Aurelianus Reomensis: A Critical Edition and Commentary."

42. *Knapp, Janet E., "The *Conductus* of the Notre Dame School."
43. *Marshall, (Mrs.) Judith Moftey, "The Repertory of the St. Martial Manuscript Paris, Bibliothèque Nationale, *fonds latin 1139.*"
44. *Smith, Norman E., "The *Clausulae* of the Notre Dame School."

RENAISSANCE

(1400-1600)

Bos

45. Allaire, Gaston Georges, "The Masses of Claudin de Sermisy." 941 pp. (Ph.D., Musicology, 1960)
    LC No.: Mic 60-3432. DA XXI.5, 1211.
46. Buker, Alden Putnam, "*Choralbearbeitung* from Johann Walther to Dietrich Buxtehude." 216 pp. (Ph.D., Musicology, 1953)
47. Key, Donald Rochester, "Two Manuscripts of Instrumental Ensemble Music from the Elizabethan Period (British Museum *Add. MS 31390* and Bodleian Library *MSS D. 212-216*)." 505 pp. in 2 vols.: Vol. II, Appendix. (Ph.D., Musicology, 1960)
    LC No.: Mic 60-3463. DA XXI.5, 1213.
48. Parks, Edna D., "English Hymns and Their Tunes in the Sixteenth and Seventeenth Centuries." 441 pp. (Ph.D., Musicology, 1957)
49. *Boucher, Joan A., "The Religious Music of Binchois."
50. *Brandon, Sanford, "The Anthems and Service Music Written for the Church of England from 1534 to 1570."
51. *Crosby, C. Russell, "The Organ Music of Hans Leo Hassler."
52. *Spiro, Arthur G., "The Five-Part Madrigals of Luzzasco Luzzaschi."
53. *Wing, Henry J., Jr., "The Polychoral Motets of Ludovico Balbi and Leone Leoni."

Brand

54. *Macomber, Bruce Barclay, "The *air de cour*, 1570-1600."

Cal B

55. Gottlieb, Louis Edward, "The Cyclic Masses of Trent Codex 89." 2 vols.: Vol. I, 209 pp., text; Vol. II, 218 pp., transcriptions. (Ph.D., Music, 1958)
56. Lyon, Margaret E., "Early Tudor Church Music: The Lambeth and Caius Manuscripts." 2 vols.: Vol. I, study; Vol. II, transcriptions. (Ph.D., Music, 1957)
57. Picker, Martin, "The Chanson Albums of Marguerite of Austria: *Manuscripts 228* and *11239* of the Bibliothèque Royale de Belgique, Bruxelles." 2 vols.: Vol. I, 515 pp., text; Vol. II, 420 pp., transcriptions. (Ph.D., Music, 1960)

58. Robinson, Sidney Charles, "The Music of the *Pepys MS 1236*." 2 vols.: Vol. I, 230 pp., text; Vol. II, 206 pp., transcriptions. (Ph.D., Music, 1959)

59. Sparks, Edgar H., "*Cantus-firmus* Treatment in Fifteenth-Century Music." 372 pp. (Ph.D., Music, 1950)

Cal LA

60. Rodgers, James Bruce, "The Madrigals of Orazio Vecchi." 990 pp. (Ph.D., Music, 1954)

Cath

61. Lefkoff, Gerald, *Five Sixteenth-Century Venetian Lute-Books: Intabolatura . . . De Diversi Autori (1563); Intabolatura . . . Di Bernardino Balletti (1554); Intabolatura . . . Dell'Eccellent P. Paulo Borrono (1563); Intabolatura . . . De Iulio Abundante (1563); and Intabolatura . . . De M. Antonio Di Becci (1568).* Washington, D. C., The Catholic University of America Press, 1960. xv, 208 pp. (Ph.D., Musicology, 1960)

Chi

62. Beikman, Donald R., "The Uses of Terms for Music: Johannes Ockeghem." iii, 109 pp. (Ph.D., Music, 1957)

63. Byler, Arthur William, "Italian Currents in the Popular Music of England in the Sixteenth Century." 206 pp. (Ph.D., Music, 1952)

64. Carpenter, Hoyle, "The Works of Antonio de Cabezón." 417 pp. (Ph.D., Music, 1957)

65. Marco, Guy A., "Zarlino on Counterpoint: An Annotated, Indexed Translation, with Introduction and Commentary, of Book III of *Le Istitutioni Harmoniche*." iii, 451 pp. (Ph.D., Music, 1956)

Clare

66. Spelman, Leslie P., "Art and the Reformation: A Critical Study of the Effects of the Protestant Reformation on the Continental Arts of the Sixteenth and Seventeenth Centuries, and in Particular on the Organ Music of France and Germany up to the Time of J. S. Bach." 284 pp. (Ph.D., Music, 1946)

Colum

67. *Cazeaux, Isabelle, "The Chansons of Claudin de Sermisy."

29

68. *Hartmann, Arnold, "Guarini's *Pastor Fido:* A History of Various Settings."
69. *Novak, Saul, "The Concept of Repetition in Fifteenth-Century Music."
70. *Siebert, F. Mark, "Liturgical Organ Music in the Fifteenth Century."

Cor

71. Barbour, James Murray, "Equal Temperament: Its History from Ramis (1482) to Rameau (1737)." 354 pp. (Ph.D., Musicology, 1932)
    Abstract in *Abstracts of Theses* (Cornell University, 1932)
72. Kendall, William Raymond, "Samuel Mareschall, His Life and Works (1554-1640)." 667 pp. (Ph.D., Musicology, 1940)
    Abstract in *Abstracts of Theses* (Cornell University, 1941)
73. Lee, Barbara, "Giovanni Maria Lanfranco's *Scintille di Musica* and Its Relation to Sixteenth-Century Music Theory." viii, 272 pp. (Ph.D., Musicology, 1961)
74. Nelson, Everett Franklin, "An Introductory Study of the English Three-Part String Fancy." 2 vols.: Vol. I, 798 pp., text; Vol. II, 292 pp., music. (Ph.D., Musicology, 1960)
    LC No.: Mic 60-2263. DA XXI.1, 205.
75. *Rosen, Ida, "The Treatment of Dissonance in the Works of Josquin des Prez and His Contemporaries."

Flor

76. Hughes, John Gillian, Jr., "The *Tientos, Fugas,* and *Diferencias* in the *Obras de música para tecla, arpa y vihuela* of Antonio de Cabezón." 182 pp. (Ph.D., Music Theory, 1961)
77. Spratt, John F., "The Masses of Antoine de Févin." 568 pp. in 2 vols. (Ph.D., Music Theory, 1960)
    LC No.: Mic 60-1418. DA XX.11, 4403.
78. *Murphy, (Mrs.) Catherine, "Transcription and Study of Two Canzonet Collections of Thomas Morley, 1597-1598." (Music Education)

Harv

79. Brown, Howard Mayer, "The Chanson in the French Theater of the Fifteenth and Early Sixteenth Centuries: Moralities, Farces, *Sotties,* and Monologues." 821 pp. in 2 vols. (Ph.D., Music, 1959)

80. Burns, Joseph Albert, "Neapolitan Keyboard Music from Valente to Frescobaldi." 2 vols.: Vol. I, 255 pp., text, and 25 pp., 13 plates, Appendices A-D; Vol. II, 142 pp., music. (Ph.D., Music, 1953)

81. Carapetyan, Armen, "The *Musica Nova* of Adriano Willaert, With a Reference to the Humanistic Society of Sixteenth-Century Venice." 2 vols.: Vol. I, 300 pp., text; Vol. II, 38 pp., music. (Ph.D., Music, 1945)
    Summary in *Summaries of Theses . . . 1943-1945* (Harvard University, 1947), pp. 540-543.

82. D'Accone, Frank A., "A Documentary History of Music at the Florentine Cathedral and Baptistry in the Fifteenth Century." 2 vols.: Vol. I, 314 pp., text; Vol. II, 255 pp., appendix of documents. (Ph.D., Music, 1960)

83. Goldthwaite, Scott, "Rhythmic Patterns and Formal Symmetry in the Fifteenth-Century Chanson." 2 vols.: Vol. I, 393 pp., text; Vol. II, 78 pp., music. (Ph.D., Music, 1956)

84. Haar, James E., "*Musica mundana:* Variations on a Pythagorean Theme." vi, 558 pp. (Ph.D., Music, 1961)

85. Haigh, Andrew C., "The Harmony of Palestrina." 324 pp. (Ph.D., Music, 1946)

86. Heartz, Daniel L., "Instrumental Music and the Dance in the French Renaissance." 424 pp. (Ph.D., Music, 1957)

87. Helm, Everett B., "The Beginnings of the Italian Madrigal and the Works of Arcadelt." xlvii, 331 pp. in 2 vols. (Ph.D., Music, 1939)
    Summary in *Summaries of Theses . . . 1939* (Harvard University, 1942), pp. 288-293.

88. Hibberd, Lloyd, "The Early Keyboard Prelude: A Study in Musical Style." 385 pp., text, and 66 unnumbered pp., music. (Ph.D., Music, 1941)
    Summary in *Summaries of Theses . . . 1941* (Harvard University, 1945), pp. 381-385.

89. Hoppin, Richard Hallowell, "The Motets of the Early Fifteenth-Century *Manuscript J.II.9* in the Biblioteca Nazionale of Turin." 2 vols.: Vol. I, 391 pp., text; Vol. II, 223 pp., music. (Ph.D., Music, 1952)

90. Kaufman, Henry W., "The Life and Works of Nicola Vicentino." 2 vols.: Vol. I, iv, 396 pp., text and bibliography; Vol. II, 443 pp., music supplement. (Ph.D., Music, 1960)

91. Keller, Walter B., "The Italian Organ Hymn from Cavazzoni to Aresti: A Study of the Interrelation of Roman Plainchant and Liturgical Keyboard Music of the Sixteenth and Seven-

teenth Centuries." 466 pp., text; 146 pp., music supplement. (Ph.D., Music, 1958)

92. Miller, Hugh Milton, "English Plainsong Compositions for Keyboard in the Sixteenth Century." 2 vols.: Vol. I, 306 pp., text; Vol. II, 308 pp., music. (Ph.D., Music, 1943)

Summary in *Summaries of Theses . . . 1943-1945* (Harvard University, 1947), pp. 530-532.

93. Moe, Lawrence Henry, "Dance Music in Printed Italian Lute Tablature from 1507 to 1611." 2 vols.: Vol. I, 309 pp., text; Vol. II, 195 pp., music. (Ph.D., Music, 1956)

94. Nelson, Robert Uriel, "The Technical Development of the Instrumental Variation from Cabezón to Reger." 281 pp. (Ph.D., Music, 1944)

Summary in *Summaries of Theses . . . 1943-1945* (Harvard University, 1947), pp. 536-539.

Published as *The Technique of Variation. A Study of the Instrumental Variation from Antonio de Cabezón to Max Reger.* Berkeley and Los Angeles, The University of California Press, 1948. *University of California Publications in Music, Vol. III.* viii, 197 pp.

95. Sholund, Edgar Roy, "The *Compendium Musices* by Adrianus Petit Coclico." 2 vols.: Vol. I, 139 pp.; Vol. II, 170 pp., including photostats of the original treatise. (Ph.D., Music, 1952)

96. Slim, H. Colin, "The Keyboard Ricercar and Fantasia in Italy, *ca.* 1500-1550, with Reference to Parallel Forms in European Lute Music of the Same Period." 2 vols.: Vol. I, 378 pp., text; Vol. II, 325 pp., appendices (including transcriptions). (Ph.D., Music, 1961)

97. Sutherland, Gordon Alexander, "Studies in the Development of the Keyboard and Ensemble Ricercare from Willaert to Frescobaldi." 2 vols.: Vol. I, 434 pp., text; Vol. II, 85 pp., music. (Ph.D., Music, 1942)

Summary in *Summaries of Theses . . . 1942* (Harvard University, 1946), pp. 327-330.

98. Tuttle, Stephen Davidson, "William Byrd: A Study of the History of English Keyboard Music to 1623." 2 vols.: Vol. I, 143 pp., text; Vol. II, 97 pp., music. (Ph.D., Music 1941)

Summary in *Summaries of Theses . . . 1941* (Harvard University, 1945), pp. 385-387.

99. Wicks, John Doane, "The Motets of Pierre de Manchicourt (*ca.* 1500-1564)." 288 pp. in 2 vols. (Ph.D., Music, 1959)

100. Wilder, Robert Dinsmoor, "The Masses of Orlando di Lasso with Emphasis on His Parody Technique." 2 vols.: Vol. I, 391 pp., text; Vol. II, 97 pp., music. (Ph.D., Music 1952) UR 3060.
101. *Bonvalot, Antony, "The Popular Part-Song of Tudor England."
102. *Culley, Thomas D., S.J., "The Musical Activity of the Colleges of the Society of Jesus in Rome, ca. 1550-1600."
103. *Cummings, Winford Claude, Jr., "Pedagogic Concepts of Sixteenth-Century Composition in the Diatonic Genus."
104. This topic released.
105. *Waldbauer, Ivan, "The Cittern and Its Music in the Second Half of the Sixteenth Century."
106. *Woollen, Rev. Charles Russell, "The Mass Ordinaries of the Manuscript J.II.9 in the Biblioteca Nazionale of Turin."

Ill

107. Young, Clyde William, "The Keyboard Tablatures of Bernhard Schmid, Father and Son." 515 pp. (Ph.D., Musicology, 1957) UM 23,410. DA XVII.11, 2633.
108. *Binkley, Thomas E., "The German Polyphonic *Lied* of the Sixteenth Century."
109. *Johnson, Roy D., "The *Manuscript Banco Rari 229 (Magl. XIX, 59)* of the Biblioteca Nazionale Centrale, Florence."
110. *Snow, Robert J., "The Manuscript Prague, Strahov Monastery, *D.G.IV.47.*"

Ind

111. Atcherson, W. Thomas, "Modal Theory of Sixteenth-Century German Theorists." 178 pp. (Ph.D., Theory, 1960)
112. MacClintock, (Mrs.) Carol Cook, "The Five-Part Madrigals of Giaches de Wert." 921 pp. (Ph.D., Musicology, 1955) UM 12,838. DA XV.8, 1411.
113. Maynard, Judson, "The Editing of, and Commentary on, an Anonymous Musical Treatise of the Sixteenth Century, British Museum, *Additional MS 4911.*" 558 pp. in 2 vols. (Ph.D., Theory, 1961)
114. Mueller, Paul Edward, "The Influence and Activities of English Musicians on the Continent during the Late Sixteenth and Early Seventeenth Centuries." 604 pp. in 2 vols. (Ph.D., Musicology, 1954) UM 7534. DA XIV.4, 685.

115. Pease, Edward Joseph, "An Edition of the Pixérécourt Manuscript: Paris, Bibliothèque Nationale, *fonds fr. 15123.*" 739 pp. in 3 vols.: Vol. I, commentary; Vols. II and III, transcriptions. (Ph.D., Musicology, 1960)
    LC No.: Mic 60-2831. DA XXI.4, 922.

116. Rogers, Helen Olive, "The Development of a Concept of Modulation in Theory from the Sixteenth to the Early Eighteenth Century." 482 pp. (Ph.D., Theory, 1955)
    UM 14,665. DA XVI.2, 351.

117. Salop, Arnold, "The Masses of Jacob Obrecht (1450-1505), Structure and Style." 621 pp. in 2 vols.: Vol. I, commentary; Vol. II, musical examples. (Ph.D., Musicology, 1959)
    LC No.: Mic 59-4034. DA XX.6, 2325.

118. Trumble, Ernest Lorenz, "Early Renaissance Harmony." 302 pp. (Ph.D., Theory, 1954)
    UM 10,159. DA XIV.11, 2089.

119. *Birmingham, Hugh M., "The Genesis and Development of the German Polyphonic *Lied* up to the Year 1500." (Musicology)

120. *Brown, Samuel E., Jr., "The Motet, 1400-1475." (Musicology)

121. *Caird, (Mrs.) Armida, "A Stylistic Analysis of the Motets of Jacob Obrecht." (Musicology)

122. *Gerken, Robert, "The Polyphonic Setting of the Proper of the Mass: Its History and Development from the Trent Codices to Isaac's *Choralis Constantinus.*" (Musicology)

123. *Hasenflug, (Mrs.) Laura Kennedy, "*Benjamin Cosyn's Virginal Book* (British Museum: *Royal Library MS 23.L4*): Transcription and Commentary." (Musicology)

Iowa

124. Clendenin, William Ritchie, "The Use of the French Chanson in Some Polyphonic Masses by French and Netherlands Composers, 1450-1550." 2 vols.: Vol. I, xi, 454 pp., commentary; Vol. II, vii, 371 pp., transcriptions. (Ph.D., Musicology, 1952)
    UR 676.

125. Feese, Gerald, "The Polyphonic Ballades in the Manuscript Torino, Biblioteca Nazionale, *J.II.9.*" 2 vols.: Vol. I, ix, 357 pp., commentary; Vol. II, lxx, 339 pp., transcriptions. (Ph.D., Musicology, 1959)
    LC No.: Mic 59-5709. DA XX.6, 2322.

126. Wienandt, Elwyn A., "Musical Style in the Lute Compositions of Francesco da Milano (1498-1543)." 2 vols.: Vol. I, xi, 140

pp., commentary; Vol. II, 239 pp., thematic index and transcriptions. (Ph.D., Musicology, 1951)

UR 3055.

127. *Dempster, Fred E., "The Magnificat Settings of Orlando di Lasso." (Musicology)

128. *Turrentine, Herbert C., "The Instrumental Fantaisies of François-Eustache du Caurroy (1549-1609)." (Musicology)

Mich

129. Barber, Elinore Louise, "Antonio de Cabezón's *cantus-firmus* Compositions and Transcriptions." 3 vols.: Vol. I, 232 pp., commentary; Vol. II, 288 pp., documents, MSS, etc.; Vol. III, 246 pp., music. (Ph.D., Music, 1960)

LC No.: Mic 60-1737. DA XX.12, 4678.

130. Biggle, Lloyd, Jr., "The Masses of Antoine Brumel." 439 pp. (Ph.D., Musicology, 1953)

UM 5760. DA XIII.5, 831.

131. Bruinsma, Henry A., "The *Souterliedekens* and Its Relation to Psalmody in the Netherlands." 588 pp. (Ph.D., Musicology, 1949)

UM 1160. DA IX.1, 148.

132. Buggert, Robert W., "Alberto da Ripa: Lutenist and Composer." 440 pp. (Ph.D., Music, 1956)

UM 21, 154. DA XVII.6, 1350.

133. Collins, Walter Stowe, "The Anthems of Thomas Weelkes." 2 vols.: Vol. I, 215 pp., commentary; Vol. II, 279 pp., music. (Ph.D., Music, 1960)

LC No.: Mic 60-6853. DA XXI.8, 2317.

134. Flower, John Arnold, "Giovanni Gabrieli's *Sacrae Symphoniae* (1597)." 370 pp. in 2 vols. (Ph.D., Music, 1956)

UM 21,136. DA XVII.6, 1351.

135. Lovell, John Harrison, "The Masses of Josquin des Prez." 520 pp. (Ph.D., Music, 1960)

LC No.: Mic 60-2548. DA XXI.2, 351.

136. Miller, Clement Albin, "The *Dodecachordon* of Heinrich Glarean." 871 pp. in 2 vols. (Ph.D., Musicology, 1951)

UM 2424. DA XI.2, 375.

137. Minor, Andrew C., "The Masses of Jean Mouton." 755 pp. in 2 vols. (Ph.D., Musicology, 1951)

UM 2364. DA XI.2, 376.

138. Pearson, Frank Cogswell, Jr., "The Madrigals of Peter Philips." 423 pp. in 2 vols. (Ph.D., Musicology, 1961)

139. Rigsby, Oscar Lee, "The Sacred Music of Elzéar Genet." 679

pp. in 2 vols.: Vol. I, historical and analytical study; Vol. II, edition of selected works. (Ph.D., Musicology, 1955)
UM 11,346. DA XV.4, 605.

140. Warren, Edwin Brady, "The Masses of Robert Fayrfax." 643 pp. (Ph.D., Musicology, 1952)
UM 3814. DA XII.4, 433.

141. *Bastian, James George, Jr., "The Sacred Music of Claudio Merulo."

142. *Lappan, Patricia, "The Music of *Padre* Manuel Rodrigues Coelho."

143. *McKinley, Ann Watson, "The Motets of Francesco Corteccia."

144. *Nuernberger, Louis Dean, "The Five-Voiced Madrigals of Cipriano de Rore."

145. *Skei, Allen Bennet, "The *Moralia* of Jacob Handl."

146. *Van Solkema, Sherman, "The Sacred Music of Pierre Certon."

N Car

147. Davis, Bertran, "The Works of Johannes Vincenet." xiii, 164 pp., text; 386 pp., musical supplement. (Ph.D., Music, 1960)

148. Fouse, Donald, "The Sacred Music of Giammateo Asola." 188 pp., text; 76 pp., musical supplement. (Ph.D., Music, 1960)

149. Hansen, Peter Sijer, "The Life and Works of Dominico Phinot (*ca.* 1510- *ca.* 1555)." iv, 115 pp. Musical supplement on file in Music Department Library. (Ph.D., Music, 1939)

150. Howell, Almonte C., Jr., "The French Organ Mass in the Sixteenth and Seventeenth Centuries." 334 pp., text; 60 pp., musical supplement. (Ph.D., Music, 1953)
UR 1476.

151. McPeek, Gwynn S., "The Windsor Manuscript, British Museum, *Egerton 3307.*" vi, 147 pp. Musical supplement on file in Music Department Library, 130 pp. (Ph.D., Music, 1950)

152. Pruett, (Mrs.) Lilian Pibernik, "The Masses and Hymns of Costanzo Porta." v, 159 pp., text; 274 pp., musical supplement. (Ph.D., Music, 1960)

153. *Bernstein, Melvin, "The Liturgical Music of Giaches Wert."

154. *Gates, Earl William, "The Masses of Johannes Martini."

155. *Kottick, Edward Leon, "The Music of the *Chansonnier Cordiforme*: Paris, Bibliothèque Nationale, *fonds fr. 1.5.13.*"

156. *Mixter, Keith, "Johannes Brassart and His Works."

157. *Monschein, Robert Winfield, "The German Chorale in the Work of Michael Praetorius."

158. *Satterfield, John R., Jr., "The Vocal Works of Christopher Tye."

159. *Strassler, Paul Gene, "Diego Ortiz: Hymns for the Church Year and Other Sacred Choral Works."

N Tex

160. Lawes, Robert Clement, Jr., "The *Seville Cancionero* [Biblioteca Colombina, *MS 7-1-28*]: Transcription and Commentary." 384 pp.; 4 illus. (Ph.D., Musicology, 1960)
161. McKee, William Elmer, "The Music of Florentio Maschera (1540-1584)." ix, 409 pp. (Ph.D., Musicology, 1958) LC No.: Mic 58-7251. DA XIX.6, 1405.
162. Shipp, Clifford M., "A Chansonnier of the Dukes of Lorraine: The Paris Manuscript *fonds français 1597*." 580 pp.; 3 plates. (Ph.D., Musicology, 1960)
163. *Newton, Paul G., "A Chansonnier of the Florence Conservatory: *MS Mus. 2439 (Codex Basevi)*." (Musicology)
164. *Nugent, William, "The Collected Works of Antonius Divitis (b. *ca*. 1475)." (Musicology)
165. *Parton, Kenton, "*Cantus-firmus* Techniques in the Organ Works of the Early Tudor Period." (Musicology)

N Wes

166. Ballard, William Joseph, "The Sources, Development, and Culmination of the Dramatic Madrigal." v, 234 pp. (Ph.D., Music, 1957) UM 24,894. DA XVIII.3, 1061.
167. Howerton, George Russell, "A Comparative Study of Performance Style in Choral Literature from the Renaissance to the Modern Period." 194, x pp. (Ph.D., Music, 1950)
168. Lincoln, Harry B., "Annibale Zoilo: The Life and Works of a Sixteenth-Century Italian Composer." 129 pp. (Ph.D., Music, 1951)
169. Tegnell, John Carl, Jr., "Elizabethan Musical Prosody: A Study of the Style of the English Madrigal and Ayre." 222 pp. (Ph.D., Music, 1948)
170. Wade, Walter Wilson, "The Sacred Style of Luca Marenzio as Represented in His Four-Part Motets, 1585." 313 pp. in 2 vols. (Ph.D., Music History and Literature, 1958) LC No.: Mic 59-231. DA XX.2, 692.

NY Gr

171. Brooks, Catherine, "Antoine Busnois as a Composer of Chansons." 2 vols.: Vol. I, 195 pp., text; Vol. II, 332 pp., transcriptions. (Ph.D., Music, 1951)

172. Lawry, Eleanor McChesney, "The Psalm Motets of Claude Goudimel." 234 pp. (Ph.D., Music, 1954)
    UM 11,939. DA XV.6, 1082.

173. Lyder, (Mrs.) Péguy S., "The Latin Sacred Music of Peter Philips." 660 pp. (Ph.D., Music, 1955)
    UM 24,790. DA XVIII.2, 607.

174. Main, Alexander, "Costanzo Festa: The Masses and Motets." 331 pp. (Ph.D., Music, 1960)

175. Marshall, George Ruffin, "The Harmonic Laws in the Madrigals of Carlo Gesualdo." 211 pp. (Ph.D., Music, 1956)
    UM 16,774. DA XVI.7, 1260.

176. Michael, George Albert, "The Parody Mass Technique of Philippe de Monte." 342 pp. in 2 vols. (Ph.D., Music, 1959)
    LC No.: Mic 59-2449. DA XX.2, 689.

177. Schuetze, George C., Jr., "The Works of Guillaume Faugues." 365 pp. (Ph.D., Music, 1960)
    LC No.: Mic 60-2304. DA XXI.1, 207.
    Published in three separate volumes as follows:

    An Introduction to Faugues by George C. Schuetze, Jr. Brooklyn, New York, Institute of Mediaeval Music, 1960. *Musicological Studies, Vol. 2.* 94 pp.
    Collected Works of Faugues, ed. George C. Schuetze, Jr. Brooklyn, New York, Institute of Mediaeval Music, 1960. *Collected Works, No. 1.* 178 pp.
    Opera Omnia Faugues: Facsimile of the Compositions of Faugues from the Manuscripts Trent 88—Trent 91, Cappella Sistina 14, Cappella Sistina 51, Verona DCCLXI, Modena α. M. 1. 13. With an Introduction by George C. Schuetze, Jr. Brooklyn, New York, Institute of Mediaeval Music, 1959. *Publications of Mediaeval Musical Manuscripts, No. 7.* 109 pp.

178. Shine, Josephine M., "The Motets of Jean Mouton." 344 pp. (Ph.D., Music, 1953)

179. Southern, (Mrs.) Eileen J., "The Buxheim Organ Book." 369 pp. in 2 vols.: Vol. I, commentary; Vol. II, selected transcriptions. (Ph.D., Music, 1961)

180. Spector, Irwin, "Robert White, Composer: Between Two Eras." 256 pp. (Ph.D., Music, 1952)

181. Steinhardt, Milton, *Jacobus Vaet and His Motets*. East Lansing, Michigan State University Press, 1951. vii, 189 pp. (Ph.D., Music, 1950)

182. Thomson, James C., "The Works of Caron: A Study in Fif-

teenth-Century Style." 633 pp. in 2 vols. (Ph.D., Music, 1959)

LC No.: Mic 59-6346. DA XX.8, 3326.

183. Ward, John M., "The *Vihuela de Mano* and Its Literature (1536-1576)." 490 pp., text; 50 pp., musical examples. (Ph.D., Music, 1953)

184. *Cannon, Clawson Y., Jr., "The Organ Mass in the Sixteenth and Seventeenth Centuries: A Study in Musical Style."

185. *Clinkscale, Edward, "The Complete Works of Antoine de Févin."

186. *Cross, Ronald, "The Complete Works of Matthaeus Pipelare."

187. *Jacobs, Charles, "The Performance Practice of Spanish Renaissance Keyboard Music."

188. *Schmidt, Liselotte, "The Italian Secular Works of Jachet Berchem."

NY Ed

189. Kabis, *Sister* Mary Elise, "The Works of Jean Richafort, Renaissance Composer (1480?-1548)." 2 vols.: Vol. I, 232 pp., text; Vol. II, 543 pp., transcriptions. (Ph.D., Music Education, 1957)

UM 22,741. DA XVII.12, 3038.

190. *Morse, Dorothy, "Word Painting and Symbolism in the Secular Choral Works of Thomas Weelkes."

Peab

191. Carruth, Carroll D., "Antoine de Bertrand: French Chromatic-Chanson Composer of the Sixteenth Century." vi, 380 pp. (Ph.D., Music, 1961)

192. *Sokol, Thomas A., "Music and Verse in Two Eclogues of Juan del Encina."

Penn

193. Bethel, Walter Leroy, "The Burgundian Chanson (1400-1477): A Study in Musical Style." 204 pp. (Ph.D., Musicology, 1950)

UM 2367. DA XI.2, 372.

194. Boyd, Morrison Comegys, *Elizabethan Music and Musical Criticism.* Philadelphia, University of Pennsylvania Press, 1940. xi, 347 pp. (Ph.D., Music, 1932)

195. Eldridge, Muriel Tilden, "Thomas Campion (1567-1620): His Poetry and Music; A Study in Relationships." 179 pp. (Ph.D., Musicology, 1958)

LC No.: Mic 58-3321. DA XIX.4, 829.

Prin

196. Hamm, Charles Edward, "A Chronology of the Works of Guillaume Dufay, Based on a Study of Mensural Practice." iv, 287 pp. (Ph.D., Music, 1960) LC No.: Mic 60-4996. DA XXI.6, 1585.

197. Kerman, Joseph W., "The Elizabethan Madrigal: A Comparative Study." 3 vols.: Vols. I and II, 540 pp., text and bibliography; Vol. III, 48 pp., examples. (Ph.D., Music, 1950)

198. Levy, Kenneth J., "The Chansons of Claude Le Jeune." 356 pp. (Ph.D., Music, 1955) UM 13,705. DA XV.11, 2234.

199. Lockwood, Lewis Henry, "The Counter-Reformation and the Sacred Music of Vincenzo Ruffo." 2 vols.: Vol. I, vi, 382 pp., text and bibliography; Vol. II, 89 pp., music. (Ph.D., Music, 1960)

200. *Kellman, Herbert, "Illuminated Music Manuscripts from the Hapsburg-Burgundy Courts (1480-1530)."

Rad

201. Hewitt, Helen Margaret, "*Harmonice Musices Odhecaton*, the First Printed Collection of Part-Music (Venice: Petrucci, 1501), Transcribed into Modern Notation, Edited, and with a Commentary." 2 vols.: Vol. I, xliv, 83, 3 pp., text + 4 plates; Vol. II, 206 pp., transcriptions. (Ph.D., Music, 1938)
Published as *Harmonice Musices Odhecaton: A*, ed. Helen Hewitt; edition of the literary texts by Isabel Pope. Cambridge, Mass., The Mediaeval Academy of America, 1942; 2nd ed., 1946. 421 pp.

202. Horsley, Imogene, "The Variation before 1580." 2 vols.: Vol. I, 167 pp., text; Vol. II, 127 pp., music. (Ph.D., Music, 1954)

203. *Chapman, (Mrs.) Catherine Weeks, "Andrea Antico."

204. *Gombosi, (Mrs.) Marilyn Purnell, "The Life and Works of Giovanni Giacomo Gastoldi."

Roch

205. Bezdeck, *Sister* John Joseph, "The Harmonic and Contrapuntal Style of Orlando Lasso." 2 vols.: Vol. I, 420 pp., commentary; Vol. II, 108 pp., music. (Ph.D., Theory, 1946) UR 1542.

206. Burton, Martin C., "Changing Concepts of Rhythm in English Musical Writings, 1500-1740." 386 pp. (Ph.D., Musicology, 1956)

207. Cuyler, Louise Elvera, "The *Choralis Constantinus Book III* of Heinrich Isaac (*ca.* 1445-1517)." 3 vols.: Vol. I, 122 pp., commentary; Vols. II and III, 395 pp., transcriptions. (Ph.D., Musicology, 1948)

Published as *Heinrich Isaac's Choralis Constantinus Book III.* Transcribed from the Formschneider First Edition (Nürnberg, 1555) by Louise Cuyler. Ann Arbor, The University of Michigan Press, 1950. *University of Michigan Publications: Fine Arts, Vol. II.* 456 pp.

208. Denker, Fred Herman, "A Study of the Transition from the *cantus-firmus* Mass to the Parody Mass." 357 pp. in 2 vols. (Ph.D., Musicology, 1951)

UR 860.

209. Dittmer, Alma, "The Vocal Polyphony of William Byrd." 372 pp. in 2 vols. (Ph.D., Theory, 1950)

210. Grauer, Albert W., "The Vocal Style of Sixt Dietrich and Johann Eccard and Their Contributions to Lutheran Church Music." 199 pp., text; 144 pp., musical supplement. (Ph.D., Theory, 1960)

211. Halvorson, Lynnette, "The *Lieder* of Ludwig Senfl." 230 pp., text; 246 pp., musical supplement. (Ph.D., Theory, 1959)

212. Jarvis, *Sister* Mary Eloise, "The Latin Motets of Hans Leo Hassler." 3 vols.: Vol. I, 278 pp.; Vol. II, 101 pp.; Vol. III, 134 pp. (Ph.D., Theory, 1959)

213. Kimmel, William B., "Polychoral Music and the Venetian School." 2 vols.: Vol. I, 165 pp., commentary; Vol. II, 111 pp., transcriptions of representative motets in score. (Ph.D., Musicology, 1942)

UR 1676.

214. Oberg, Paul Matthews, "The Sacred Music of Philippe de Monte." 2 vols.: Vol. I, 381 pp., commentary; Vol. II, 219 pp., transcriptions of one mass and 24 motets. (Ph.D., Musicology, 1944)

215. Spurbeck, Samuel Wayne, "A Study of the Canonici Manuscript *Misc. 213* (*ca.* 1400-1440)." 2 vols.: Vol. I, 102 pp., commentary; Vol. II, 445 pp., transcriptions. (Ph.D., Musicology, 1943)

UR 2699.

216. Stein, Edwin Eugene, "The Polyphonic Mass in France and the Netherlands, *ca.* 1525 to *ca.* 1560." 2 vols.: Vol. I, 238 pp., commentary; Vol. II, parts 1-4, 544 pp., transcriptions. (Ph.D., Musicology, 1941)

UR 2719.

217. Tadlock, Ray J., "The Early Madrigals of Alessandro Striggio."
2 vols.: Vol. I, 135 pp., commentary; Vol. II, 184 pp., transcriptions. (Ph.D., Musicology, 1959)

218. Warner, Richard Lyman, "The Vocal and Instrumental Technique of Orlando Gibbons." 618 pp. in 4 vols. (Ph.D.,
Theory, 1949)

219. Watanabe, Ruth T., "Five Italian Madrigal Books of the Late
Sixteenth Century: A Transcription and Study of the First
Books à cinque by Antonio Il Verso, Bartolomeo Roy, Ber-
nardino Scaramella, Pietro Paolo Quartieri, and Emilio
Virgelli." 6 vols.: Vol. I, 208 pp., commentary; Vols. II-VI,
transcriptions of madrigals in score. (Ph.D., Musicology,
1951)
UR 2979.

220. Watkins, Glenn E., "Three Books of Polyphonic Lamentations
of Jeremiah, 1549-1564." 484 pp. (Ph.D., Musicology, 1953)
UR 2980.

221. Woldt, John W., "Spanish Madrigals: A Study of the Madrigals
of Morales, Flecha, Valenzola, Brudieu, and Rimonte." 2
vols.: Vol. I, 135 pp., commentary; Vol. II, 3 vols. in one,
136, 56, 58 pp., transcriptions of madrigals. (Ph.D., Musicology, 1950)

222. Young, Edward, "The Contrapuntal Practices of Victoria." 381
pp. (Ph.D., Theory, 1942)

223. *Haldeman, William, "The Vocal Compositions of Christian
Erbach." (Musicology)

224. *Sparks, Dan C., "Reymann's Noctes Musicae." (Musicology)

225. This topic released.

226. *Weidner, Robert Wright, "The Early In Nomine: A Genesis
of Chamber Music." (Musicology)

S Cal

227. Barnett, Howard, "Factors in the Transition from Renaissance
to Baroque in English Music." 330 pp. (Ph.D., Music, 1958)

228. Borrowdale, George, "The Musices Liber Primus of Diego Ortiz,
Spanish Musician." 1086 pp. in 3 vols.: Vols. I and II, text;
Vol. III, music. (Ph.D., Musicology, 1952)

229. Bright, Robert Houston, "The Early Tudor Part-Song from
Newarke to Cornyshe." 463 pp. (Ph.D., Musicology, 1952)

230. Riedel, Johannes, "Leisen Formulae: Their Polyphonic Settings
in the Period of the Renaissance and Reformation." 1166 pp.:
675 pp., text; 42 pp., bibliography; 449 pp., musical examples. (Ph.D., Musicology, 1953)

231. Trotter, Robert M., "The Franco-Flemish Chanson of Thomas Crecquillon." iv, 502 pp. (Ph.D., Musicology, 1957) UR 2871.

232. Young, Irwin, "Franchinus Gafurius, Theorist and Composer." iv, 372 pp. (Ph.D., Musicology, 1954)

233. *Daniels, Arthur, "The *De Musica Libri VII* of Francisco de Salinas."

234. *Johnson, Milton, "The Psalter of the Sixteenth and Seventeenth Centuries."

235. *Lamont, Herbert Barry, "The Music of John Shepherd (d. 1563)."

Stan

236. Vaught, Raymond, "The Fancies of Alfonso Ferrabosco II." 2 vols.: Vol. I, ix, 282 pp., text; Vol. II, iv, 200 pp., has title 'The Unpublished Fancies' (scores). (Ph.D., Music, 1959)

Tor

237. King, John Reymes, "An Aesthetic and Musical Analysis of the Madrigals of Thomas Morley, with Special Reference to Relations between Text and Music and Some Comparison with the Madrigals of John Wilbye, John Bennet, and the *Triumphs of Oriana.*" xxvi, 616 pp. (Ph.D., Music, 1950)

U Theol

238. Duerksen, Rosella Reimer, "Anabaptist Hymnody of the Sixteenth Century: A Study of Its Marked Individuality, Coupled with a Dependence on Contemporary Secular and Sacred Musical Style and Form." iii, 276 pp. (D.S.M., 1956)

239. Giuliana, Paul, "History and Development of Magnificat Settings in the Fifteenth and Sixteenth Centuries." 63 pp. (D.S.M., 1950)

240. Hamersma, John Edward, "*Les Dix Pseaumes* of Claude Le Jeune: A Study in Sixteenth-Century French Psalmody." 2 vols.: Vol. I, 188 pp., commentary; Vol. II, 271 pp., transcriptions of the *10 Pseaumes.* (D.S.M., 1961)

241. *Boehringer, James, "The Earliest Collections of Lutheran Music."

Wash StL

242. Adams, Robert Lee, "The Development of a Keyboard Idiom in England during the English Renaissance." 3 vols.: Vol. I, 147 pp., text; Vol. II, 64 pp., transcription of *Royal App. 56;*

Vol. III, thematic index of English virginal MSS (about 60 MSS). (Ph.D., Musicology, 1960)

Wisc

243. Sromovsky, Robert Albert, "Giovanni Animuccia, 15—-1571." 258 pp. (Ph.D., Music, 1936)

244. Wagner, Lavern John, "The *Octo Missae* of George de La Hèle, 1547-1587." 2 vols.: Vol. I, 289 pp., analysis; Vol. II, 513 pp., transcriptions. (Ph.D., Music, 1957)
    UM 22,435. DA XVII.10, 2282.

245. *Gray, Walter B., "A Comparison of the Latin and English Sacred Choral Compositions of William Byrd."

W Res

246. *Lehmann, Arnold O., "The Liturgical Music of the Lutheran Church in the First Century of the Lutheran Church (1520-1620): Its Sources and Development and Its Influence upon Church and Sacred Music."

Yale

247. Johnson, Alvin H., "The Liturgical Music of Cipriano da Rore." 355 pp. (Ph.D., History of Music, 1954)

248. Kenney, Sylvia W., "The Works of Walter Frye." 442 pp. (Ph.D., History of Music, 1955)

249. Kirby, Frank, "Hermann Finck's *Practica Musica:* A Comparative Study in Sixteenth-Century Musical Theory." 305 pp. (Ph.D., History of Music, 1957)

250. Lerner, Edward Robert, "The Sacred Music of Alexander Agricola." 1106 pp. in 4 vols.: Vol. I, 410 pp., text; Vols. II-IV, 696 pp., music. (Ph.D., History of Music, 1958)

251. Lord, Robert Sutherland, "The Buxheim Organ Book: A Study in the History of Organ Music in Southern Germany during the Fifteenth Century." 257 pp. (Ph.D., History of Music, 1960)

252. Mattfeld, (Mrs.) Jacquelyn Anderson, "*Cantus firmus* in the Liturgical Motets of Josquin des Prez." 165 pp., text; 77 plates; 92 pp., transcriptions. (Ph.D., History of Music, 1959)

253. Mattfeld, Victor H., "Georg Rhaw's Publications for Vespers: A Study of Liturgical Practices of the Early Reformation." 544 pp. in 2 vols. (Ph.D., History of Music, 1960)

254. Miller, (Mrs.) Catharine Ann Keyes, "A Fifteenth-Century Record of English Choir Repertory: British Museum *Add.*

MS 5665; A Transcription and Commentary." 309 pp. in 2 vols. (Ph.D., History of Music, 1948)

255. Murphy, Richard M., "Fantasia and Ricercare in the Sixteenth Century." 222 pp. (Ph.D., History of Music, 1954)

256. *Simson, Walter H., "The Motets of Andrea Gabrieli."

BAROQUE ERA
(1600-1750)

Bos

257. Glowacki, John, "The History of Polish Opera." 220 pp. (Ph.D., Musicology, 1952)
258. Green, Douglass Marshall, "The Instrumental Ensemble Music of Leonardo Leo against the Background of Contemporary Neapolitan Music." 290 pp. (Ph.D., Musicology, 1958)
      LC No.: Mic 58-3099. DA XIX.4, 829.
259. Holmes, Robert William, "The Use of *contrafacta* in the Large Choral Works of J. S. Bach." 423 pp. (Ph.D., Musicology, 1960)
      LC No.: Mic 60-3459. DA XXI.4, 922.
260. Jaffé, Angela Maria, "The Cantatas of Johann Ludwig Bach." 542 pp. (Ph.D., Musicology, 1957)
261. Podolsky, Saul, "The Variation Canzona for Keyboard Instruments in Italy, Austria, and Southern Germany in the Seventeenth Century." 201 pp. (Ph.D., Musicology, 1954)
262. *Davis, Richard C., "Self Parody among the Cantatas of Johann Sebastian Bach."
263. *Fagerholm, Lillian, "The Sacred Vocal Works of Henry Purcell."
264. *King, William J., "The English Anthem and Its Culmination in Handel's Chandos Anthem."

Brand

265. *Burrows, David L., "The Cantatas of Antonio Cesti."

Cal B

266. Duckles, Vincent Harris, "John Gamble's Commonplace Book: A Critical Edition of New York Public Library *MS Drexel 4257.*" 1013 pp. (Ph.D., Music, 1953)
267. *Jackson, Roland H., "Giovanni Maria Trabaci of Naples as a Composer of Vocal and Instrumental Music."

Cal LA

268. Carfagno, Simon A., "The Life and Dramatic Music of Stefano Landi with a Transliteration and Orchestration of the Opera *Sant' Alessio.*" 2 vols. in 4: Vol. I, 508 pp., text; Vol. II, 269 folios, musical score. (Ph.D., Music, 1960)

269. Ittenberg, Uriel M., "The Fugues of J. S. Bach: A Study of Their Structure, Style, and Texture." 363 pp. (Ph.D., Music, 1956)

270. Meltzer, Eugene, "The Secular Songs of Henry Purcell." 179 pp. (Ph.D., Music, 1957)

271. *Biales, Albert, "Johann Rosenmüller's Music for Instrumental Ensembles."

272. *Stone, Kenneth Gordon, "The Oratorios of Alessandro Stradella and His Modenese Contemporaries."

Cath

273. Connor, *Sister* M. John Bosco, *Gregorian Chant and Mediaeval Hymn-Tunes in the Works of J. S. Bach.* Washington, D. C., The Catholic University of America Press, 1957. xii, 187 pp. (Ph.D., Musicology, 1957)

274. Foelber, Paul Frederick, *Bach's Treatment of the Subject of Death in His Choral Music.* Washington, D. C., The Catholic University of America Press, 1961. 435 pp. (Ph.D., Musicology, 1961)

275. Keane, *Sister* Michaela Maria, *The Theoretical Writings of Jean-Philippe Rameau.* Washington, D. C., The Catholic University of America Press, 1961. 265 pp. (Ph.D., Musicology, 1961)

276. *Ardry, Roger, "The Influence of the Choral Writing of Giacomo Carissimi on the Oratorios of Georg Friedrich Handel."

277. *Leddy, Margaret, "A Stylistic Analysis of the Masses and Motets of Antonio Lotti (1667-1740)."

278. *Weirauch, Jean S., "The Violoncello Sonata Literature in France during the Eighteenth Century."

Colum

279. Myers, Robert M., *Handel's "Messiah," a Touchstone of Taste.* New York, Macmillan Co., 1948. 338 pp. (Ph.D., Musicology, 1948)

280. Rowen, Ruth H., *Early Chamber Music.* New York, King's Crown Press, 1949. 188 pp. (Ph.D., Musicology, 1950)

281. *Holmes, William, "*Buffo* Elements in Seventeenth-Century Italian Opera."

282. *Mulder, George, "Simon Stevin's *Van de Spiegeling der Singconst.*"

283. *Newman, Joel, "Salomone Rossi's Madrigals."

284. *Thiemann, Susan, "The Vocal Duet in the First Half of the Seventeenth Century."

285. *Williams, Hermine, "Francesco Bartolomeo Conti: His Life and Works."

Cor

286. Poladian, Sirvart, "Handel as an Opera Composer." 481 pp. (Ph.D., Musicology, 1946)
Abstract in *Abstracts of Theses* (Cornell University, 1946)
LC No.: Mic 58-2779. DA XIX.8, 2101.

287. *Samuel, Harold E., "The Cantata in Nuremberg during the Seventeenth Century."

Flor

288. Agey, Calvin Buell, "A Study of the *Kleine geistliche Concerte* and *Geistliche Chormusik* of Heinrich Schütz." 2 vols.: Vol. I, 209 pp., commentary; Vol. II, 203 pp., musical examples. (Ph.D., Music Theory, 1955)
UM 11,191. DA XV.3, 429.

289. Barnes, Marysue, "The Trio Sonatas of Antonio Caldara." 509 pp. in 2 vols. (Ph.D., Music Theory, 1960)
LC No.: Mic 60-1403. DA XX.11, 4405.

290. Murphy, Arthur Loring, "The *Bicinia Variorum Instrumentorum* of Johann Christoph Pezel." 425 pp. in 2 vols. (Ph.D., Music Education, 1959)
LC No.: Mic 59-1761. DA XX.2, 690.

291. Rhea, Claude H., Jr., "The Sacred Oratorios of Georg Philipp Telemann (1681-1767)." 406 pp. in 2 vols.: Vol. I, An Historical and Stylistic Survey; Vol. II, A Selected Anthology of Music. (Ed.D., Music Education, 1958)
LC No.: Mic 58-5995. DA XIX.8, 2102.

292. *DeLage, Joseph Ovide, Jr., "The Opera Overture to 1750." (Music Theory)

293. *Farley, Charles Edward, "The Organ Concerti of Georg Friedrich Handel." (Music Theory)

294. *Meyer, Ramon Eugene, "John Playford's *An Introduction to the Skill of Musick:* A Study of All the Editions and Revisions from 1654 to 1730." (Music Theory)

Harv

295. Aldrich, Putnam Calder, "The Principal *agréments* of the Seventeenth and Eighteenth Centuries: A Study in Musical Orna-

mentation." cxxviii, 719 pp. in 3 vols. (Ph.D., Music, 1942)
> Summary in *Summaries of Theses . . . 1942* (Harvard University, 1946), pp. 324-330.

296. Barber, Clarence Howard, "The Liturgical Music of Marc-Antoine Charpentier (1634-1704): The Masses, Motets, *Leçons de Ténèbres.*" 2 vols.: Vol. I, 477 pp., text; Vol. II, 228 pp., music. (Ph.D., Music, 1955)

297. Barwick, Steven, "Sacred Vocal Polyphony in Early Colonial Mexico." 2 vols.: Vol. I, 220 pp., text; Vol. II, 274 pp., music. (Ph.D., Music, 1949)

298. Beveridge, Lowell Pierson, "Giacomo Carissimi: A Study of His Life and His Music with Latin Texts in the Light of the Institutions Which He Served and through the Perspective of Liturgical, Literary, and Musical Theory and Practice." 3 vols.: Vols. I and II, 510 pp., text; Vol. III, 132 pp., music. (Ph.D., Music, 1944)
> Summary in *Summaries of Theses . . . 1943-1945* (Harvard University, 1947), pp. 533-536.

299. Clarke, Henry Leland, "John Blow (1649-1708), Last Composer of an Era." 4 vols.: Vols. I-III, 860 pp., text; Vol. IV, 122 pp., music. (Ph.D., Music, 1947)

300. Coopersmith, Jacob Maurice, "An Investigation of Georg Friedrich Händel's Orchestral Style." 12 vols.: Vol. I, 187 pp., text; Vols. II-XII, 4114 pp., "A Thematic Index of the Printed Works of Georg Friedrich Händel." (Ph.D., Music, 1932)
> Summary in *Summaries of Theses . . . 1932* (Harvard University, 1934), pp. 318-319.

301. Grout, Donald J., "The Origins of the *opéra-comique.*" 5 vols.: Vols. I and II, 402 pp., text; Vols. III-V, 97, 143, 181 pp., supplements. (Ph.D., Music, 1939)
> Summary in *Summaries of Theses . . . 1939* (Harvard University, 1942), pp. 286-288.

302. Hughes, Royal Delaney, "The French Influence on Bach." 125 pp. (Ph.D., Music, 1926)
> Summary in *Summaries of Theses . . . 1926* (Harvard University, 1930), pp. 199-201.

303. Jones, Vincent Lloyd, "The Relation of Harmonic Theory and Practice from Rameau to 1900." 648 pp. in 2 vols. (Ph.D., Music, 1934)
> Summary in *Summaries of Theses . . . 1934* (Harvard University, 1935), pp. 362-366.

304. Mishkin, Henry George, "The Function of the Episodic Se-

quence in Baroque Instrumental Music." 175 pp. (Ph.D., Music, 1938)

    Summary in *Summaries of Theses . . . 1938* (Harvard University, 1940), pp. 367-368.

305. Ohl, John Franklin, "The Orchestration of Bach's Vocal Works." 4 vols.: Vols. I and II, 579 pp., text; Vol. III, 144 pp., tables; Vol. IV, 48 unnumbered pages, music examples. (Ph.D., Music, 1945)

    Summary in *Summaries of Theses . . . 1943-1945* (Harvard University, 1947), pp. 543-546.

306. Palisca, Claude V., "The Beginnings of Baroque Music: Its Roots in Sixteenth-Century Theory and Polemics." 399 pp. (Ph.D., Music, 1954)

307. Woodward, Henry Lynde, "A Study of the Tenbury MSS of Johann Pachelbel." 2 vols.: Vol. I, 360 pp., text; Vol. II, 241 pp., music. (Ph.D., Music, 1952)

308. *Bonta, Stephen, "The Instrumental Music of Giovanni Legrenzi."

309. *Fuller, David R., "A Survey of French Keyboard Music from Rameau to the Revolution."

310. *Jander, Owen H., "The Works of Alessandro Stradella Related to the Cantata and the Opera."

311. *Mead, Ernest C., Jr., "The Music of Girolamo Frescobaldi."

Ill

312. Ahnell, Emil Gustave, "The Concept of Tonality in the Operas of Jean-Philippe Rameau." 293 pp. (Ph.D., Musicology, 1957)

    UM 25,188. DA XVIII.2, 605.

313. *Curtis, Alan S., "English Elements in Dutch Secular Music of the Early Seventeenth Century."

314. *Willheim, Imanuel, "Johann Adolph Scheibe: German Musical Thought in Transition."

Ind

315. Bolen, Charles Warren, "Open-Air Music of the Baroque: A Study of Selected Examples of Wind Music." 264 pp. (Ph.D., Music Education, 1954)

    UM 8778. DA XIV.8, 1232.

316. Bowman, Horace B., "A Study of the *castrati* Singers and Their Music." 157 pp. (Ph.D., Music Education, 1952)

317. Haynes, Maurice Brooks, "The Keyboard Works of Bernardo

Pasquini (1637-1710)." 970 pp. in 4 vols. (Ph.D., Musicology, 1960)
LC No.: Mic 60-2820. DA XXI.3, 639.

318. Morris, Robert Bower, "A Study of the Italian Solo Cantata before 1750." 197 pp. (Mus. Ed.D., 1955)
UM 14,300. DA XV.11, 2234.

319. Smith, Charles Samuel, "Leonhard Euler's *Tentamen novae theoriae musicae:* A Translation and Commentary." 365 pp. (Ph.D., Theory, 1960)
LC No.: Mic 60-2844. DA XXI.3, 642.

320. Speer, Klaus, "A Portuguese Manuscript of Keyboard Music from the Late Seventeenth Century: *MS No. 1607, Loc. G,* 7, Municipal Library, Oporto, Portugal." 2 vols.: Vol. I, xv, 112 pp., commentary; Vol. II, 230 pp., transcriptions. (Ph.D., Musicology, 1956)
UM 17,979. DA XVI.12, 2477.

321. Wessel, Frederick T., "The *Affektenlehre* in the Eighteenth Century." 433 pp. (Ph.D., Musicology, 1955)
UM 14,674. DA XVI.1, 134.

322. Whaples, (Mrs.) Miriam Karpilow, "Exoticism in Dramatic Music, 1600-1800." 415 pp. (Ph.D., Musicology, 1958)
LC No.: Mic 58-7938. DA XIX.11, 2975.

323. Wise, Wayne Wilmar, "Tonal Relationship through Interchangeability of Mode in the Music of the Eighteenth and Nineteenth Centuries." 245 pp. (Ph.D., Theory, 1956)
UM 19,480. DA XVII.3, 647.

324. *Danek, (Mrs.) Lillie Lohman, "Modulation in Recitatives of Choral Works, 1600-1800." (Theory)

325. *Egan, (Mrs.) Anne-Marie, "Minor French Theorists of the Eighteenth Century." (Theory)

326. *Egan, John B., "Mersenne's *Traité de l'harmonie universelle,* Book II: Translation and Critical Commentary."

327. *Hauptfuehrer, George, "The Harpsichord Suites of Handel in Relation to Keyboard Suites of Some of His Predecessors and Contemporaries." (Theory)

328. *Hudson, Barton, "A Study of the *Libro de Cyfra.*" (Musicology)

329. *Knowlton, Jean, "Some Dances of the Stuart Masque Identified and Analyzed." (Musicology)

330. *Krehbiel, James W., "The Criticism of Rameau's Theoretical Works by His Contemporaries."

331. *Leavitt, Donald, "The Rise of Monody in English Church Music." (Musicology)

332. *Lewin, Harold F., "A Stylistic Study of the Madrigals of Monteverdi." (Theory)
333. *Marcase, Donald, "A Study of Handel's Chandos Anthems: Their Influence on the Development of His Later Oratorio Style." (Musicology)
334. *Morey, Carl, "The Late Operas of Alessandro Scarlatti." (Musicology)
335. *Patton, H. Lloyd, "The *Devisen-Arie*." (Musicology)
336. *Rayner, Clare, "Two Little-Known Seventeenth-Century English Composers: Christopher Gibbons and Benjamin Rogers." (Musicology)
337. *Sargent, George, "Critical Analysis of *Elizabeth Rogers' Virginal Book* (1656)." (Musicology)
338. *Smith, Helen M., "*Il Trionfo della Practica Musicale* by Francesco Maria Veracini: Translation and Commentary." (Musicology)
339. *Swenson, Milton, "A Study of the Ensemble Ricercar in the Baroque Era." (Musicology)

Iowa

340. Bock, Emil W., "The String Fantasies of John Hingeston (*ca.* 1610-1683)." 2 vols.: Vol. I, xi, 251 pp., commentary; Vol. II, ii, 287 pp., thematic index and transcriptions. (Ph.D., Musicology, 1956)
    UM 16,106. DA XVI.5, 969.
341. *Dean, Robert H., Jr., "The Instrumental Compositions of Michel Mascitti *(ca.* 1664-1760): An Italian Influence on French Music." (Musicology)
342. *Dunn, James P., "The *Grands Motets* of Marc-Antoine Charpentier (1634-1704)." (Music)
343. *Lynch, Howard L., "The Transcription Technique of J. S. Bach in His Original Instrumental Works." (Theory)
344. *Schmidt, Warren F., "The Organ Works of Johann Gottfried Walther (1684-1748)." (Theory)

Mich

345. Borroff, Edith, "The Instrumental Works of Jean-Joseph Casanéa de Mondonville." 2 vols.: Vol. I, 351 pp., commentary; Vol. II, 55 pp., an edition of his Opus V, *Pièces de clavecin avec voix ou violon* (1748). (Ph.D., Music, 1959)
    LC No.: Mic 59-2099. DA XIX.12, 3319.
346. Bryden, John Rennie, "The Motets of Orazio Benevoli." 578 pp. in 2 vols. (Ph.D., Musicology, 1951)
    UM 2576. DA XI.3, 701.

347. Cavanaugh, Robert William, "The Anthems in *Musica Deo Sacra* by Thomas Tomkins." 468 pp. (Ed.D., Music Education, 1953)
UM 5649. DA XIII.5, 832.
348. Giebler, Albert Cornelius, "The Masses of Johann Caspar Kerll." 391 pp. in 2 vols. (Ph.D., Musicology, 1957)
LC No.: Mic 58-919. DA XVIII.4, 1453.
349. Hitchcock, Hugh Wiley, "The Latin Oratorios of Marc-Antoine Charpentier." 900 pp. (Ph.D., Musicology, 1954)
UM 7663. DA XIV.4, 684.
350. McArtor, Marion E., "Francesco Geminiani, Composer and Theorist." 387 pp. (Ph.D., Musicology, 1951)
UM 2363. DA XI.2, 374.
351. Preston, Robert Elwyn, "The Forty-Eight Sonatas for Violin and Figured Bass of Jean-Marie Leclair, *l'aîné.*" 656 pp. (Ph.D., Music, 1959)
LC No.: Mic 59-4972. DA XX.5, 1821.
352. Rarig, Howard Raymond, Jr., "The Instrumental Sonatas of Antonio Vivaldi." 455 pp. (Ph.D., Musicology, 1958)
LC No.: Mic 58-7779. DA XIX.6, 1406.
353. Reddick, Harvey Phillips, "Johann Mattheson's Forty-Eight Thorough-Bass Test-Pieces: Translation and Commentary." 327 pp. in 2 vols. (Ph.D., Music, 1956)
UM 19,715. DA XVII.1, 152.
354. Reilly, Edward Randolph, "Johann Joachim Quantz's *Versuch einer Anweisung die Flöte traversiere zu spielen:* A Translation and Study." 879 pp. in 2 vols.: Vol. I, translation; Vol. II, study. (Ph.D., Musicology, 1958)
LC No.: Mic 59-4974. DA XXI.1, 207.
355. Stillings, Frank Stuart, "Arcangelo Corelli." 356 pp. (Ph.D., Music, 1956)
UM 19,715. DA XVII.1, 153.
356. Thompson, Clyde H., "The Music of Marin Marais." 628 pp. (Ph.D., Music, 1957)
LC No.: Mic 58-1006. DA XVIII.4, 1454.
357. Vogan, Charles E., "The French Organ School of the Seventeenth and Eighteenth Centuries." 422 pp. (Ph.D., Musicology, 1949)
UM 1358. DA IX.3, 152.
358. Warner, Robert Austin, "The Fantasia in the Works of John Jenkins." 331 pp. in 2 vols. (Ph.D., Musicology, 1951)
UM 2365. DA XI.2, 378.
359. *Bartholomew, Leland, "Italian Instrumental Ensemble Music of the Early Seventeenth Century."

360. *Castle, Conan, "The Motets of André Campra."
361. *Farndell, Gordon H., "The Organ Magnificat in the Seventeenth Century."
362. *MacDonald, John A., "The Sacred Works of Legrenzi."
363. *Mackey, Elizabeth Jocelyn, "The Sacred Works of Johann Theile."
364. *Soluri, James Joseph, "The Sacred Music of Lodovico Grossi da Viadana."
365. *Somer, Avo, "The Keyboard Works of Froberger."

Minn

366. *Schuler, *Rev.* Richard J., "The Sacred Works of Giovanni Maria Nanino."

N Car

367. Beswick, Delbert Meacham, "The Problem of Tonality in Seventeenth-Century Music." xii, 341 pp. (Ph.D., Music, 1951) UR 318.
368. Jordan, Henry Bryce, "The Music of Pelham Humfrey." 401 pp. (Ph.D., Music, 1956)
369. Klenz, William, "The Life and Works of Giovanni Maria Bononcini." iv, 276 pp., text; 283 pp., musical supplement. (Ph.D., Music, 1958)
    LC No.: Mic 59-50. DA XIX.11, 2972.
370. Lehn, Edgar vom, "The Sacred Cantatas of Philipp Heinrich Erlebach (1657-1714)." 230 pp. (Ph.D., Music, 1958)
    LC No.: Mic 58-5973. DA XIX.8, 2104.
371. Livingston, Herbert, "The Italian Overture from A. Scarlatti to Mozart." 343 pp., text; vii, 198 pp., musical supplement. (Ph.D., Music, 1952)
    UR 1809.
372. Mason, Wilton E., Jr., "The Lute Music of Sylvius Leopold Weiss." vii, 124 pp. Musical supplement on file in Music Department Library. (Ph.D., Music, 1950)
373. Monroe, James Frank, "Italian Keyboard Music in the Interim between Frescobaldi and Pasquini." xvi, 166 pp., text; 109 pp., musical supplement. (Ph.D., Music, 1959)
    LC No.: Mic 59-6440. DA XX.7, 2838.
374. Nelson, Philip F., "Nicolas Bernier: A Study of the Man and His Music." 5 vols.: Vol. I, ix, 270 pp., text; Vols. II-V, unpaginated musical supplement. (Ph.D., Music, 1958)
    LC No.: Mic 59-53. DA XIX.11, 2972.

375. Sites, Caroline O., "Benedetto Marcello's Chamber Cantatas." iv, 128 pp. (Ph.D., Music, 1959)
LC No.: Mic 59-6448. DA XX.7, 2839.

376. Weaver, Robert Lamar, "Florentine Comic Operas of the Seventeenth Century." xii, 366 pp. Musical supplement on file in Music Department Library. (Ph.D., Music, 1958)
LC No.: Mic 58-5975. DA XIX.8, 2104.

377. *Clarke, Mary Gray, "Francesco Maria Veracini's Life and Works."

378. *Fred, Herbert W., "The Instrumental Music of Johann Christof Pepusch."

379. *Henderson, Hubert, "The Music of John Wilson."

380. *Huber, Calvin, "The Instrumental Music of William Brade."

381. *Mitchell, Harris, "The Works of Antonio Giuseppe Brescianello."

382. *Pruett, James Worrell, "The Works of Filippo Vitali."

383. *Shannon, John R., "The *Mylauer Tabulaturbuch* of 1750."

384. *Williams, Nyal, "The Sacred Works of Marco da Gagliano."

N Tex

385. Kelton, Raymond H., "The Instrumental Music of Ascanio Mayone." 381 pp. (Ph.D., Musicology, 1961)

386. *Douglass, Robert S., "The Keyboard Ricercar in the Baroque Era." (Musicology)

387. *Streetman, R. David, "The Life and Works of Christoph Bernhard (1627-1692)." (Musicology)

N Wes

388. Eickhoff, Henry John, "The Ritornello Principle in the Organ Works of Johann Sebastian Bach." 524 pp. in 2 vols.: Vol. I, study; Vol. II, appendix. (Ph.D., Music History and Literature, 1960)
LC No.: Mic 60-4749. DA XXI.5, 1212.

389. Jones, William John, "The Literature of the Transverse Flute in the Seventeenth and Eighteenth Centuries." xiv, 519 pp. (Ph.D., Music, 1952)

390. Nolte, Ewald Valentin, "The Instrumental Works of Johann Pachelbel (1653-1706): An Essay to Establish His Stylistic Position in the Development of the Baroque Musical Art." 360 pp. (Ph.D., Music, 1954)
UM 9264. DA XIV.10, 1758.

391. Parsons, Pleasants Arrand, "Dissonance in the Fantasias and So-natas of Henry Purcell." 208 pp. (Ph.D., Music, 1953) UM 6233. DA XIII.6, 1218.

392. Wattenbarger, James Albert, "The *Turmmusik* of Johann Pe-zel." 298 pp. (Ph.D., Music, 1957) UM 24,932. DA XVIII.2, 609.

393. *Beck, Theodore Albert, "The Organ Chorales of Johann Gott-fried Walther: An Analysis of Style." (Theory)

394. *Brundrett, Grant Allen, "The Orchestration of Rameau." (Mu-sic History and Literature)

395. *Gatza, Thaddeus R., "The Musical Ideas of Johann Mattheson and Their Background." (Music History and Literature)

396. *Hotaling, Edward Roy, "William Croft: His Music." (Theory)

397. *Pankratz, Herbert Raymond, "The Male Voice in German Choral Music in the Baroque Era." (Music History and Lit-erature)

398. *Waldschmidt, Carl Luther, "The Works of Georg Boehm." (Music History and Literature)

399. *Willis, Thomas Creighton, "Monteverdi's *L'Incoronazione di Poppea:* A Contribution to the History of Performance Practice." (Music History and Literature)

NY Gr

400. Cohen, Albert, "The Evolution of the Fantasia and Works in Related Styles in the Seventeenth-Century Instrumental En-semble Music of France and the Low Countries." 304 pp. (Ph.D., Music, 1959) LC No.: Mic 59-2440. DA XX.3, 1038.

401. Pearl, Mildred, "The Suite in Relation to Baroque Style." 286 pp. (Ph.D., Music, 1957) UM 24,880. DA XVIII.2, 607.

402. *Below, George, "Johann David Heinichen's *Der General-Bass in der Composition:* A Translation and Critical Study."

403. *Cherry, Norman, "The North Italian Trumpet Repertory, 1665-1720."

404. *Golos, Jerzy, "Organ Music in Poland before 1750."

405. *Warner, Thomas, "Indications of Performance Practice in Woodwind Methods of the Seventeenth and Eighteenth Centuries."

Peab

406. Funk, Floyd D., "The Trio Sonatas of Georg Philipp Telemann (1681-1767)." 320 pp. (Ph.D., Music, 1954)

Penn

407. Klitenic, Zelik, "The *clavecin* Works of Jean-Philippe Rameau." 353 pp. (Ph.D., Musicology, 1955) UM 13,399. DA XV.12, 2541.

408. Morgan, Catharine, "The Bach Fugue: A Study in Antecedents." 266 pp. (Ph.D., Musicology, 1958) LC No.: Mic 58-3362. DA XIX.4, 831.

409. Rotondi, Joseph Emilio, "Literary and Musical Aspects of Roman Opera, 1600-1650." 287 pp. (Ph.D., Musicology, 1959) LC No.: Mic 59-2265. DA XX.1, 320.

Prin

410. *Freeman, Robert, "Caldara and the Arcadian Reform of the Opera."

411. *Reichlin, Gerhart, "Continental Influences on the Work of Henry Purcell."

412. *Reiner, Stuart, "From *Orfeo* to *L'Incoronazione di Poppea*."

413. *Stalnaker, William, "The Beginnings of the Neapolitan Opera."

414. *Wood, Thor E., "J. G. Walther as Lexicographer."

Rad

415. Crocker, Eunice Chandler, "An Introductory Study of the Italian Canzona for Instrumental Ensembles and Its Influence upon the Baroque Sonata." 2 vols.: 497 pp., text; 43 pp., music; 48 pp., bibliography. (Ph.D., Music, 1943)

416. *Churgin, Bathia D., "The Instrumental Music of G. B. Sammartini."

Roch

417. Baxter, William H., Jr., "Agostino Steffani: A Study of the Man and His Work." 365 pp., text; 107 pp., supplement. (Ph.D., Musicology, 1957) UR 243.

418. Fay, Robert Vernon, "The Vocal Style of Michael Praetorius." 281 pp. (Ph.D., Theory, 1946)

419. Gore, Richard Taylor, "The Instrumental Works of Georg Muffat." 260 pp. (Ph.D., Theory, 1955)

420. Miller, (Mrs.) Gertrude B., "Tonal Materials in Seventeenth-Century English Treatises." 401 pp. (Ph.D., Theory, 1960)

421. Mueller, Harold, "The *Musicalische Gespräche über die Evangelia* of Andreas Hammerschmidt." 560 pp. in 2 vols. (Ph.D., Musicology, 1956) UR 2084.

422. Munson, John Kenneth, "The *Musicalischer Seelenlust* of Tobias Michael." 577 pp. (Ph.D., Musicology, 1953)
UR 2087.

423. Presser, William, "The Fugue before Bach." 557 pp. in 2 vols. (Ph.D., Theory, 1947)

424. Proctor, George Alfred, "The Works of Nicola Matteis, Sr." 2 vols.: Vol. I, 186 pp., text; Vol. II, 138 pp., appendix of music. (Ph.D., Musicology, 1960)

425. Riley, James W., "William Gregory the Younger: Musitian of the King's Musick." 150 pp. (Ph.D., Musicology, 1959)

426. Rowell, Lewis E., Jr., "Four Operas of Antonio Vivaldi." 344 pp. (Ph.D., Theory, 1959)
UR 2499.

427. Schempf, William H., "Seventeenth-Century Magnificats." 2 vols.: Vol. I, 290 pp., text; Vol. II, 374 pp., examples. (Ph.D., Musicology, 1960)

428. Zeyen, *Sister* M. Mark, "The Development of the Functional Use of the Supertonic Seventh Chord, as Evidenced in Representative Keyboard Suites of the Seventeenth Century." 215 pp. (Ph.D., Theory, 1956)
UR 1916.

429. *Applegate, Joan S., "The Henry Lawes Autograph Manuscript: British Museum, *Loan 35*." (Musicology)

430. *Bemis, Jack, "Restoration Dramatic Music." (Theory)

431. *Buff, Iva Mary, "The Secular Cantatas of Giacomo Carissimi." (Musicology)

432. *Kooiker, Anthony, "Locke's *Melothesia:* Its Place in the History of Keyboard Music in Restoration England." (Musicology)

433. *Livingstone, Ernest F., "The State of Music Teaching in the Protestant German Schools as Evidenced by Original Source Material, Especially the Textbook Collection of Abraham Ursinus of the First Decade of the Seventeenth Century." (Musicology)

434. *McElrath, Hugh T., "Milanese Church Music in the Early Baroque." (Musicology)

435. *Sleeper, William Allen, "Harmonic Style of the English Fancy of the Commonwealth and Restoration." (Theory)

436. *Sutton, Julia, "Jean-Baptiste Bésard's *Novus Partus*." (Musicology)

437. *Walker, F. Marian, "The Music of Giovanni Coperario (John Cooper) in Theory and Practice." (Theory)

S Cal

438. Alderman, Pauline, "Anthoine Boësset and the *air de cour*." 369 pp. (Ph.D., Music, 1946)

439. Arnold, Byron, "The Life and Works of John Caspar Bachofen (1697-1755)." xiv, 434 pp. (Ph.D., Musicology, 1956)

440. Gillespie, John Edward, "The Music for Harpsichord of Nicholas Le Bègue." 339 pp., text; 148 pp., music. (Ph.D., Music, 1951)

441. Morgan, Wesley, "The Chorale Motet between 1650 and 1750." 363 pp. (Ph.D., Musicology, 1956)
    UR 2056.

442. Ray, Alice Elizabeth, "The Double-Choir Music of Juan de Padilla." 2 vols.: Vol. I, 354 pp., text and bibliography; Vol. II, 192 pp., musical examples. (Ph.D., Musicology, 1953)

443. Richards, James E., "The 'Grand Motet' of the Late Baroque in France as Exemplified by Michel-Richard de Lalande and a Selected Group of His Contemporaries." 305 pp., text; 535 pp., music. (Ph.D., Music, 1950)
    UR 2442.

444. Zimmerman, Franklin B., "Purcell's Musical Heritage: A Study of Musical Styles in Seventeenth-Century England." 463 pp., ports., music. (Ph.D., Musicology, 1958)
    LC No.: Mic 59-876. DA XX.2, 692.

445. *Barnes, Clifford R., "Music in the Repertory of the *Théâtre de la Foire*."

446. *Lee, Gerald E., "Enharmonic Practices in the Baroque Era."

Stan

447. Bicknell, (Mrs.) Joan Colleen, "Interdependence of Word and Tone in the Dramatic Music of Henry Purcell." xi, 256 pp.; illus. (music). (Ph.D., Music, 1960)

448. Houle, George Louis, "The Musical Measure as Discussed by Theorists from 1650 to 1800." vii, 311 pp.; illus. (music). (Ph.D., Music, 1960)

449. Powell, Newman Wilson, "Rhythmic Freedom in the Performance of French Music from 1650 to 1735." xviii, 382 pp.; illus. (music). (Ph.D., Music, 1958)
    LC No.: Mic 59-3719. DA XX.5, 1820.

450. Seagrave, (Mrs.) Barbara Anne Garvey, "The French Style of Violin Bowing and Phrasing from Lully to Jacques Aubert (1650-1730)." xviii, 291 pp.; illus (music). (Ph.D., Music, 1958)
    LC No.: Mic 59-1452. DA XIX.12, 3322.

Tex

451. *Farrar, Lloyd P., "Christian Huygens: His Musical Contributions to Seventeenth-Century Science."

U Theol

452. Christmann, Arthur H., "Johann Joachim Quantz on the Musical Practices of His Time." 217 pp. (D.S.M., 1950)

Wash

453. *Scandrett, Robert L., "The Anthems of William Croft (1678-1728)."

Wisc

454. Roe, Horton L., "The *Camerata de' Bardi* and the Foundations of Music Drama." 200 pp. (Ph.D., Italian and Music, 1951)
455. *Lewis, Edgar L., "Seventeenth-Century Music for Wind Instruments."

W Res

456. Fink, J. Harold, "Handel and the Doctrine of the Affections: An Analysis of the Expressive Means in Handel's Oratorios and Correlations with the Doctrine of the Affections." (Ph.D., Music, 1952)

Yale

457. Hyde, Fred B., "Mersenne as Theorist of Music." 605 pp. (Ph.D., History of Music, 1954)
458. Rose, Gloria, "The Cantatas of Carissimi." 241 pp. (Ph.D., History of Music, 1960)
459. *Clark, Willene, "Biagio Marini."
460. *Crain, Gordon F., Jr., "The Operas of Bernardo Pasquini."
461. *Hanley, Edwin H., "The *cantate da camera* of Alessandro Scarlatti."
462. *Oppenheim, Daniel P., "The Music of Andreas Hammerschmidt."
463. *Porter, William, "Italian Monody through 1610."
464. *Suess, John, "The Sonatas of Giovanni Battista Vitali."

ROCOCO AND CLASSICAL ERA
(1730-1800)

Bos

465. Horstman, Jean, "The Instrumental Music of Johann Ludwig Krebs." 314 pp. (Ph.D., Musicology, 1959) LC No.: Mic 59-3465. DA XX.4, 1387.

Brand

466. *Rosenthal, Steven, "The Dramatic Works of Méhul."

Cal B

467. Ratner, Leonard G., "Harmonic Aspects of Classic Form." 184 pp. (Ph.D., Music, 1947)
468. Simon, Edwin Julien, "The Double Exposition in Classic Concerto Form." 255 pp. (Ph.D., Music, 1954)
469. *Edwall, Harry, "Joseph Haydn's Concerti for String and Wind Instruments."

Cal LA

470. Cantrell, Byron, "Tommaso Traetta and His Opera *Sofonisba*." 256 pp. (Ph.D., Music, 1957)
471. Haag, Charles Robert, "The Keyboard Concertos of Karl Philipp Emanuel Bach." 244 pp. (Ph.D., Music, 1956)

Cath

472. Canave, Paz Corazon G., *A Re-evaluation of the Role Played by Carl Philipp Emanuel Bach in the Development of the Clavier Sonata.* Washington, D. C., The Catholic University of America Press, 1956. xv, 186 pp. (Ph.D., Musicology, 1956)

Chi

473. Lawner, George, "Form and Drama in the Operas of Joseph Haydn." 241 pp. (Ph.D., Music, 1959)
474. Revitt, Paul J., "Attitudes and Practices of Editors Who Published Settings of Traditional Airs in the British Isles between 1750 and 1850." xvi, 382 pp. (Ph.D., Music, 1956)

Colum

475. Ringer, Alexander Lothar, "The *Chasse:* Historical and Analyti-

cal Bibliography of a Musical Genre." 441 pp. (Ph.D., Musicology, 1955)
UM 11,467. DA XV.5, 843.

476. Schwarz, Boris, "French Instrumental Music between the Revolutions (1789-1830)." 370 pp. (Ph.D., Musicology, 1950)
UM 1897. DA X.4, 250.

477. *Eitel, Luise, "The Origins of the Romantic Song-Cycle."

Cor

478. Galkin, Elliott Washington, "The Theory and Practice of Orchestral Conducting since 1752." x, 650 pp. in 2 vols. (Ph.D., Musicology, 1960)

479. Gelrud, Paul Geoffrey, "A Critical Study of the French Violin School (1782-1882)." 651 pp. (Ph.D., Musicology, 1941)
Abstract in *Abstracts of Theses* (Cornell University, 1941)

480. Winesanker, Michael, "The Record of English Musical Drama, 1750-1800." 636 pp. (Ph.D., Musicology, 1944)
Abstract in *Abstracts of Theses* (Cornell University, 1944)

481. *Eddins, John M., "Opera and *Opéra Comique* in France during the Revolution and First Empire."

Flor

482. Carroll, Charles Michael, "François-André Danican-Philidor: His Life and Dramatic Art." 2 vols.: Vol. I, 454 pp., text; Vol. II, 247 pp., *Tom Jones, Comédie Lyrique en Trois Actes:* modern ed. of Philidor's *opéra comique*, with an Eng. tr. of the text. (Ph.D., Music Theory, 1960)
LC No.: Mic 60-5490. DA XXI.8, 2316.

483. *Kelly, David T., "The Instrumental Canzonas of Adriano Banchieri." (Music Education)

484. *Pound, Gomer Jeffrey, "The Clarinet Concerto to 1850." (Music Education)

Harv

485. Daniel, Ralph Thomas, "The Anthem in New England before 1800." xvii, 286 pp., text; 79 pp., music. (Ph.D., Music, 1955)

486. Downes, Edward O. D., "The Operas of Johann Christian Bach as a Reflection of the Dominant Trends in *opera seria*, 1750-1780." 1145 pp. in 2 vols. (Ph.D., Music, 1958)

487. Parrish, Carl G., "The Early Piano and Its Influence on Keyboard Technique and Composition in the Eighteenth Century." 438 pp. (Ph.D., Music, 1939)

Summary in *Summaries of Theses . . . 1939* (Harvard University, 1942), pp. 293-296.

488. Stone, David Leon, "The Italian Sonata for Harpsichord and Pianoforte in the Eighteenth Century (1730-1790)." 3 vols.: Vol. I, 274 pp., text; Vol. II, 103 pp., "Thematic Index of Sonatas by Italian Composers of the Eighteenth Century in the Collection of the Library of Congress and in the Einstein Collection of Smith College Library"; Vol. III, 197 pp., music. (Ph.D., Music, 1952)

489. Tangeman, Robert S., "The Transition Passage in Sonata-Form Movements of the Viennese Classical Period." 2 vols.: Vol. I, 234 pp., text; Vol. II, 90 unnumbered pp., music. (Ph.D., Music, 1948)

Ind

490. Abbott, William W., Jr., "Certain Aspects of the Sonata-Allegro Form in Piano Sonatas of the Eighteenth and Nineteenth Centuries." 336 pp. (Ph.D., Theory, 1956)
UM 19,454. DA XVII.4, 865.

491. DeLerma, Dominique-René, "Wolfgang Amadeus Mozart: The Works and Influences of His First Ten Years." 331 pp. (Ph.D., Musicology, 1958)
LC No.: Mic 58-7914. DA XIX.11, 2968.

492. Jesson, Ronald Francis, "Third Relationship in the Late Eighteenth and Early Nineteenth Centuries." 170 pp. (Ph.D., Theory, 1958)
LC No.: Mic 58-7921. DA XIX.9, 2358.

493. List, George Harold, "An Analysis of the Relationship of Non-Stepwise Melodic Movement to Tonality in Selected Works of W. A. Mozart." 236 pp. (Ph.D., Theory, 1954)
UM 10,151. DA XIV.11, 2087.

494. Robinson, John David, "The Vocal Canon of the Classical Era." 383 pp. (Ph.D., Musicology, 1959)
LC No.: Mic 59-4032. DA XX.4, 1388.

495. Sonnedecker, Donald Ira, "Cultivation and Concepts of Duets for Four Hands, One Keyboard, in the Eighteenth Century." 337 pp. (Ph.D., Musicology, 1953)
UM 6453. DA XIII.6, 1219.

496. *Campbell, Robert G., "The Works of Johann Gottfried Müthel (1718-1788)." (Musicology)

497. *Hackman, Willis H., "The Structural Functions of Variation and Development in the Sonata-Form Movements of Bee-

thoven: A Study of Compositional Techniques in Musical Process and Structure." (Theory)

498. *Kaplan, David, "Stylistic Trends in the Small Woodwind Ensemble from 1750 to 1825." (Theory)

499. *Marks, James B., "Harmonic Rhythm in Selected Instrumental Works from 1775 to 1850." (Theory)

Iowa

500. Menk, Gail Ellsworth, "The Symphonic Introductions of Joseph Haydn." v, 138 pp. (Ph.D., Theory, 1960)
LC No.: Mic 60-5681. DA XXI.7, 1963.

501. Van Nice, John Robert, "The Larger Sacred Choral Works of William Boyce (1710-1779): A Study and Edition of Selected Compositions for Choir and Orchestra." 687 pp. in 3 vols. (Ph.D., Music, 1956)
UM 18,563. DA XVI.11, 2180.

502. *Benton, Rita B., "Nicolas-Joseph Hüllmandel and French Instrumental Music in the Second Half of the Eighteenth Century." (Musicology)

503. *Freedman, Frederick, "The Activities of an Immigrant American Musician and Composer: Alexander Reinagle (1756-1809)." (Musicology)

504. *Stetzel, Ronald D., "The Life and Works of John Christopher Moller (d. 1803)." (Musicology)

Mich

505. Bryan, Paul Robey, Jr., "The Symphonies of Johann Vanhal." 524 pp. in 2 vols. (Ph.D., Musicology, 1956)
UM 21,134. DA XVII.6, 1350.

506. Helm, Sanford Marion, "Carl Friedrich Abel, Symphonist: A Biographical, Stylistic, and Bibliographical Study." 393 pp. (Ph.D., Musicology, 1953)
UM 5677. DA XIII.5, 833.

507. Laing, Millard Myron, "Anton Reicha's Quintets for Flute, Oboe, Clarinet, Horn, and Bassoon." 622 pp. (Ed.D., Education and Music, 1952)
UM 3697. DA XII.4, 432.

508. Pankaskie, Lewis V., "Tonal Organization in the Sonata-Form Movements in Haydn's String Quartets." 338 pp. (Ph.D., Music, 1957)
UM 21,344. DA XVII.6, 1352.

509. Weichlein, William J., "A Comparative Study of Five Settings

of Metastasio's Libretto *La Clemenza di Tito* (1734-1791)."
518 pp. (Ph.D., Music, 1956)
UM 21,371. DA XVII.6, 1353.

510. White, Joseph Addison, Jr., "The Concerted Symphonies of John Christian Bach." 576 pp. in 2 vols.: Vol. I, Analytical Study of First Movements; Vol. II, Three Symphonies in Score [Edited by Joseph Addison White, Jr.]. (Ph.D., Musicology, 1958)
LC No.: Mic 58-3750. DA XIX.8, 2104.

511. *Herman, Martin, "French Music during the Revolutionary Period."

512. *Jobe, Robert, "The Operas of Grétry."

513. *Morrell, Garland R., "The Symphonies of Franz Anton Rosetti."

514. *Sherman, Charles Henry, "The Masses of Michael Haydn."

515. *Tighe, *Sister* Alice Eugene, "The Piano Sonatas of Muzio Clementi."

N Car

516. Fruchtman, Efrim, "The Baryton Trios of Tomasini, Burgksteiner, and Neumann." 118 pp., text; 105 pp., musical supplement. (Ph.D., Music, 1960)

517. *Bostian, Richard Lee, "The Works of Rinaldo di Capua."

N Tex

518. Gibson, Oscar Iee, "The Serenades and Divertimenti of Mozart." 394 pp. (Ph.D., Musicology, 1960)
LC No.: Mic 60-2791. DA XXI.3, 638.

519. Helm, Ernest Eugene, "The Musical Patronage of Frederick the Great." xiii, 305 pp. (Ph.D., Musicology, 1958)
LC No.: Mic 58-7248. DA XIX.7, 1780.
Published as *Music at the Court of Frederick the Great.* Norman, The University of Oklahoma Press, 1960. xx, 268 pp.

520. *Hunt, Thomas Webb, "Rousseau's *Dictionnaire de Musique* (1767) in Relation to French Music in the Eighteenth Century."

N Wes

521. Chiuminatto, Anthony Lawrence, "The Liturgical Works of Baldassare Galuppi." 472 pp. in 3 vols. (Ph.D., Music History and Literature, 1959)
LC No.: Mic 59-4786. DA XX.6, 2321.

522. Orland, Henry James, "Symphonic Sound Ideals from 1750 to 1850 and Their Cultural Background." 201 pp. in 2 vols. (Ph.D., Theory, 1959)
LC No.: Mic 59-4826. DA XX.8, 3325.

NY Gr

523. *Brofsky, Howard, "The Instrumental Music of *Padre* Martini."

NY Ed

524. Carrow, Burton Stimson, "The Relation between the Mannheim School and the Music of Franz Beck, Henri Blanchard, and Pierre Gaveaux." 445 pp. in 2 vols. (Ph.D., Music Education, 1956)
UM 17,640. DA XVII.4, 866.

Peab

525. Anderson, John Drummond, "Brass Scoring Techniques in the Symphonies of Mozart, Beethoven, and Brahms." ix, 376 pp. (Ph.D., Music, 1960)
LC No.: Mic 60-5858. DA XXI.8, 2315.
526. Rossell, Denton, "The Formal Construction of Mozart's Operatic Ensembles and Finales." 694 pp. in 2 vols. (Ph.D., Music, 1955)
UM 15,473. DA XVI.2, 352.

Penn

527. *Meyer, (Mrs.) Eve Rose, "The Chamber Music of Florian Gassmann."

Prin

528. White, E. Chappell, "Giovanni Baptista Viotti and His Violin Concertos." 341 pp. in 2 vols. (Ph.D., Music, 1957)
UM 23,887. DA XVIII.1, 252.
529. *Kamien, Roger, "Sonata Form in the Clavier Sonata (1755-1775)."

Roch

530. Durham, William E., "The Harmonic Language of Mozart: A Detailed Study of Selected Late Instrumental Works." 343 pp. (Ph.D., Theory, 1957)
531. Frederick, Kurt, "The Fugue from 1750 to 1827." 363 pp., text; 120 pp., supplement. (Ph.D., Theory, 1957)
UR 1103.

532. Marek, Robert Carl, "The Use of Harmonic Patterns in Similar Sonorities in the Music of Five Composers of the Classic Period." 518 pp. in 2 vols. (Ph.D., Theory, 1959)
533. Stedman, William Preston, "Form and Orchestration in the Pre-Classical Symphony." 440 pp. (Ph.D., Theory, 1953)
   UR 2716.
534. Thompson, Verne, "Wenzel Johann Tomaschek: His Predecessors, His Life, His Piano Works." 242 pp. (Ph.D., Musicology, 1955)
   UR 2819.
535. *Carroll, Frank Morris, "An Introduction to Antonio Soler." (Theory)
536. *Kob, Walter, "The Smaller Homophonic Forms of Instrumental Music of the Period 1730 to 1830 in Relation to Theories of Music Form and Form Textbooks." (Theory)

U Theol

537. Jensen, Donald, "The Music Dramas of Johann Heinrich Rolle." (D.S.M., 1961)

Yale

538. Pauly, Reinhard G., "Michael Haydn's Latin *Proprium Missae* Compositions." 343 pp. (Ph.D., History of Music, 1956)
539. Sternfeld, Frederick William, "Goethe and Music." 237, lix pp. (Ph.D., History of Music, 1942)
540. *Stevens, Jane R., "The Keyboard Concertos of C. P. E. Bach."
541. *Wates, Roye, "Forms and Their Meaning in the Instrumental Music of Germany, 1750-1800: A Study of Contemporary Theory and Criticism."

ROMANTIC ERA
(1800-1900)

Bos

542. Shand, David A., "The Sonata for Violin and Piano from Schumann to Debussy (1851-1917)." 403 pp. (Ph.D., Music, 1948)
543. *Siegel, (Mrs.) Linda, "The Influence of Romantic Literature on Romantic Music in Germany during the First Half of the Nineteenth Century."

Cal B

544. Chusid, Martin, "The Chamber Music of Franz Schubert." (Ph.D., Music, 1961)

Cath

545. Durham, George D., *The German Concert Overture*. Washington, D. C., The Catholic University of America Press, 1957. 270 pp. (Ph.D., Musicology, 1957)
546. *Jessel, *Sister* Mary Lisa, "The Vocal Works of Peter Ritter (1763-1846)."

Chi

547. Hutchinson, William Robert, "Implication, Closure, and Interpolated Change as Exemplified in the Works of Frédéric Chopin." 236 pp. (Ph.D., Music, 1960)

Colum

548. Crosten, William L., *French Grand Opera: An Art and a Business*. New York, King's Crown Press, 1948. 162 pp. (Ph.D., Musicology, 1947)
549. Newlin, Dika, *Bruckner, Mahler, Schönberg*. New York, King's Crown Press, 1947. 293 pp. (Ph.D., Musicology, 1945)
550. *Haft, (Mrs.) Virginia G., "Luigi Cherubini, Symphonist."
551. *Herrmann, William, "Religion in the Verdi Operas."
552. *Mell, Albert, "Paganini: Criticism, Life, and Works."

Cor

553. Longyear, Rey M., "D. F. E. Auber: A Chapter in the History of the *Opéra Comique*, 1800-1870." 439 pp. (Ph.D., Musicology, 1957)
    UM 22,202. DA XVII.9, 2027.

554. Mintz, Donald Monturean, "The Sketches and Drafts of Three of Felix Mendelssohn's Major Works." 2 vols.: Vol. I, 497 pp., text; Vol. II, 151 pp., music. (Ph.D., Musicology, 1960)

555. *Haupt, Helen, "Styles and Techniques in Piano-Playing, 1800-1825."

556. *Stringham, Ronald Scott, "The Masses of Franz Schubert."

Flor

557. Montague, Richard Addison, "Charles Edward Horn: His Life and Works (1786-1849)." 212 pp. (Ed.D., Music Education, 1959)
LC No.: Mic 59-6921. DA XX.8, 3325.

558. Wilcox, James H., "The Symphonies of Anton Bruckner." 337 pp. (Ph.D., Music Theory, 1956)
UM 18,675. DA XVI.11, 2180.

Harv

559. Yellin, Victor, "The Life and Operatic Works of George Whitefield Chadwick." 308 pp.; 113 plates. (Ph.D., Music, 1957)

Ill

560. *Garlington, Aubrey S., "The Fantastic in Dramatic Music of the Early Romantic Period, 1790-1848."

561. *Kearns, William Kay, "Horatio Parker and Music in America, 1885-1920."

Ind

562. Earl, Don Lee, "The Solo Song-Cycle in Germany (1800-1850)." 251 pp. (Ph.D., Musicology, 1952)
UM 4371. DA XII.6, 799.

563. Nordgren, Quentin Richards, "Texture: A Consideration of Spacing, Doubling, Range, and Instrumentation, Based upon Selected Orchestral Works of Certain Nineteenth-Century Composers." 388 pp. (Ph.D., Theory, 1955)
UM 12,843. DA XV.8, 1413.

564. *Ellis, Mildred Katharine, "The Piano Character-Piece and Its Treatment by French Composers of the Nineteenth Century." (Musicology)

565. *Haenselman, Carl, "Harmonic Rhythm in Selected Works of the Latter Half of the Nineteenth Century." (Theory)

566. *Hanna, Albert Lyle, "A Stylistic Analysis of the Instrumental Works of Schubert." (Theory)

567. *McGinnis, Francis, "A Stylistic Analysis of the Complete Works of Frédéric Chopin." (Theory)
568. *Murphy, Edward, "A Stylistic Analysis of the Large Orchestral Works of Richard Strauss." (Theory)
569. *Ruetz, Robert G., "The Development of the German *Lied* through an Analytical Examination of Songs with Goethe Texts." (Music Education)

Iowa

570. Luntz, George Edward, "Musical and Literary Expression in Songs from Goethe's *Wilhelm Meister*." iii, 238 pp., text; 68 pp., supplement of musical examples. (Ph.D., Music, 1953)
   UM 6532. DA XIV.1, 151.

Mich

571. Chase, Howard Randolph, "Tonality and Tonal Factors in the Piano Sonatas of Beethoven." 178 pp. (Ph.D., Musicology, 1953)
   UM 5021. DA XIII.3, 408.
572. *Liddell, (Mrs.) Charlotte Farrow, "Musical Activity at the Court of Ludwig II, 1864-1869."

N Car

573. Sasser, William, "The Guitar Music of Fernando Sor." xi, 177 pp. (Ph.D., Music, 1960)

N Wes

574. Burkholder, Samuel R., "The Oratorio: Its Development since the Time of Mendelssohn." 200, xi pp. (Ph.D., Music, 1938)
575. Ganz, Peter Felix, "The Development of the Etude for Pianoforte." 430 pp. (Ph.D., Music History and Literature, 1960)
576. Mitchell, Francis Humphries, "The Piano Concertos of Johann Nepomuk Hummel." 264 pp. (Ph.D., Music, 1957)
   UM 23,529. DA XVII.12, 3041.

NY Gr

577. Kravitt, Edward F., "The Late Romantic *Lied:* Performance, Literary Approach, and the Naturalistic Movement." 315 pp. (Ph.D., Music, 1960)

NY Ed

578. D'Ecclesius, *Rev.* Gennaro A., "The Aria Technique of Giacomo Puccini." 264 pp. (Ph.D., Music Education, 1961)

579. Doyle, John G., "The Piano Music of Louis Moreau Gott-schalk." 179 pp. (Ph.D., Music Education, 1960)

580. Jones, Arthur E., "The Choruses in the Operas of Richard Wag-ner: A Study of the Massed Vocal Ensemble in Music Drama." vi, 248 pp. (Ph.D., Music Education, 1957)
   UM 22,728. DA XVII.11, 2630.

Prin

581. Naegele, Philipp Otto, "August Wilhelm Ambros: His Histori-cal and Critical Thought." 486 pp. in 2 vols. (Ph.D., Music, 1956)
   UM 20,143. DA XVII.6, 1351.

582. *Satz, Arthur, "The Operas of Hector Berlioz."

583. *Steinberg, Michael, "Spontini's Later Operas."

Roch

584. Campbell, Douglas G., "George W. Chadwick: His Life and Works." 363 pp. (Ph.D., Theory, 1957)
   UR 552.

585. Carroll, *Mother* Catherine Agnes, "Percy Goetschius, Theorist and Teacher." 180 pp. (Ph.D., Theory, 1957)

586. Finney, Charles H., "British Theorists of the Nineteenth Cen-tury." 274 pp. (Ph.D., Theory, 1957)

587. Guenther, Ralph Russell, "Vincent d'Indy." 3 vols.: Vols. I and II, 380 pp., text; Vol. III, 170 pp., supplement. (Ph.D., Theory, 1948)

588. Hoffman, Mark, "A Study of German Theoretical Treatises of the Nineteenth Century." 268 pp. (Ph.D., Theory, 1953)

589. Kent, Charles, "Tonal Expansion in the Early Romantic Period." 325 pp. (Ph.D., Theory, 1951)
   UR 1652.

590. Kopp, Frederic, "Arthur Foote: American Composer and Theorist." 427 pp., text; 134 pp., supplement. (Ph.D., Theory, 1957)
   UR 1717.

591. Montgomery, Merle, "A Comparative Analysis [and Transla-tion] of Vincent d'Indy's *Cours de composition musicale.*" 7 vols.: Part One, translation: Book One, 371 pp. in one vol.; Book Two, Part One, 799 pp. in 3 vols.; Book Two, Part Two, 572 pp. in 2 vols. Part Two, comparative analysis: 156 pp. in one vol. (Ph.D., Theory, 1946)

592. Packard, Donald, "Seven French Theorists of the Nineteenth Century." 322 pp. (Ph.D., Theory, 1952)
   UR 2203.

593. Steunenberg, Thomas B., "Rhythmic Continuity in Slow Movements from Beethoven's Symphonies." 419 pp. (Ph.D., Theory, 1954)

594. Warch, Willard F., "A Study of the Modulation Technique of Beethoven." 2 vols.: Vol. I, vi, 208 pp.; Vol. II, charts (pages not numbered). (Ph.D., Theory, 1955)

595. Wilkinson, Harry, "The Vocal and Instrumental Technique of Charles Villiers Stanford." 2 vols.: Vol. I, 240 pp., text; Vol. II, 208 pp., musical examples. (Ph.D., Theory, 1959)

596. Will, Roy Templeton, "A Stylistic Analysis of the Works of Moussorgsky." 189 pp. (Ph.D., Theory, 1949)

597. *Miller, John, "Edward MacDowell: A Critical Study." (Theory)

S Cal

598. *Menstell, Dolores, "E. T. A. Hoffmann and Carl Maria von Weber as Critics of Music."

599. *Perkins, Marion, "Changing Concepts of Rhythm in the Piano Music of the Romantic Era."

U Theol

600. *Alviani, Doric, "The Sacred Compositions of Arthur Foote."

Wash StL

601. Schuller, Kenneth Gustave, "*Verismo* Opera and the Verists." 193 pp., text; 310 pp., supplement: annotated score of *Tosca*. (Ph.D., Musicology, 1960)

W Res

602. *Fischer, Egbert W., "Rhythm and Movement in Beethoven."

Yale

603. Selden, (Mrs.) Margery J. Stomne, "The French Operas of Luigi Cherubini." 457, xvii pp. (Ph.D., History of Music, 1951)

TWENTIETH CENTURY

Bos

604. Slepian, Dorothy, "The Use of Polyphonic Forms and Devices by Contemporary American Composers." 352 pp. (Ph.D., Music, 1946)
605. Wolf, Henry S., "The Twentieth-Century Piano Sonata." 587 pp. (Ph.D., Music, 1957)
606. *Bobbitt, Richard, "The Harmonic Idiom in the Works of the French Six."

Cal LA

607. Fenyo, Thomas, "The Piano Music of Béla Bartók." 293 pp. (Ph.D., Music, 1956)
608. Gordon, (Mrs.) Diane Kestin, "Folklore in Modern English Opera." 267 pp., text; 80 pp., music. (Ph.D., Music, 1959)
609. Hunt, Charles B., "The American Wind Band: Its Function as a Medium in Contemporary Music." 277 pp. (Ph.D., Music, 1949)
610. Langlie, Warren M., "Arnold Schoenberg as a Teacher." 200 pp. (Ph.D., Music, 1960)
611. *Philips, Mary K., A Study of Recitative in Contemporary Opera."

Cath

612. Klein, *Sister* Mary Justina, *The Contribution of Daniel Gregory Mason to American Music.* Washington, D. C., The Catholic University of America Press, 1957. xii, 154 pp. (Ph.D., Musicology, 1957)
613. *Cliff, Charles Joseph, "George Gershwin's *Porgy and Bess.*"
614. *Jenkins, Joseph Willcox, "An Analytical Survey of the Symphonies of Jean Sibelius."
615. *McBrier, Vivian Flagg, "The Life and Works of Robert Nathaniel Dett."

Colum

616. *Hatch, Christopher, "Concepts of Tonality in the Twentieth Century."

Cor

617. Bergsagel, John D., "The National Aspects of the Music of

Ralph Vaughan Williams." 329 pp. (Ph.D., Musicology, 1957)

UM 22,194. DA XVII.9, 2026.

618. Dustin, William Dale, "Two-Voiced Textures in the *Mikrokosmos* of Béla Bartók." 335 pp. (Ph.D., Musicology, 1959) LC No.: Mic 60-609. DA XX.9, 3768.

Flor

619. *Boda, Daniel, "A Study of the Works of Charles Griffes." (Music Theory)

620. *Brown, Malcolm J., "The Symphonies of Sergei Prokofiev." (Music Theory)

621. *Canfield, John Clair, "A Study of the Life and Works of Henry Hadley." (Music Education)

622. *Morris, Victor J., "The Songs of Claude Debussy." (Music Theory)

Harv

623. Austin, William W., "Harmonic Rhythm in Twentieth-Century Music." 179 pp. (Ph.D., Music, 1951)

624. Clapp, Philip Greeley, "Modern Tendencies in Musical Form." 328 pp. (Ph.D., Music, 1911)

625. Cooper, Grosvenor William, "An Introduction to the Analysis of Certain Contemporary Harmonic Practices." 74 pp., text; 48 unnumbered pp., music. (Ph.D., Music, 1939)

Summary in *Summaries of Theses . . . 1939* (Harvard University, 1942), pp. 280-283.

626. Davison, Archibald Thompson, "The Harmonic Contribution of Claude Debussy." 131 pp. (Ph.D., Music, 1908)

627. *Archibald, R. Bruce, "Harmony in the Music of Alban Berg."

628. This topic released.

629. *Crawford, John C., "The Relationship of Text and Music in the Vocal Works of Schoenberg, 1908-1925."

Ind

630. Appleby, David Percy, "A Study of Selected Compositions by Contemporary Brazilian Composers." 230 pp. (Ph.D., Theory, 1956)

UM 19,457. DA XVII.2, 372.

631. Morrison, Donald Nauman, "Influences of Impressionist Tonality on Selected Works of Delius, Griffes, Falla, and Respighi:

Based on the Concept Developed by Robert Mueller." 168 pp. (Ph.D., Theory, 1960)
LC No.: Mic 60-2829. DA XXI.3, 641.

632. Mueller, Robert Earl, "The Concept of Tonality in Impressionist Music: Based on the Works of Debussy and Ravel." 171 pp. (Ph.D., Theory, 1954)
UM 10,153. DA XIV.11, 2088.

633. Ogdon, Wilbur Lee, "Series and Structure: An Investigation into the Purpose of the Twelve-Note Row in Selected Works of Schoenberg, Webern, Krenek, and Leibowitz." 341 pp. (Ph.D., Theory, 1955)
UM 14,663. DA XVI.2, 351.

634. Walker, Mark Fesler, "Thematic, Formal, and Tonal Structure of the Bartók String Quartets." 387 pp. (Ph.D., Theory, 1955)
UM 14,672. DA XV.12, 2543.

635. *Gillespie, Frederick, "Tonality in the String Quartets of Arnold Schoenberg." (Theory)

636. *Gould, Glen, "The Twelve Tone Works of Dallapiccola." (Theory)

637. *Hanna, James, "The Symphonic Works of Arthur Honegger." (Theory)

638. *Jones, William M., "The Music of Ernest Bloch: A Study of the Evolution of a Style." (Theory)

639. *Marshall, Richard, "The Musico-Dramatic Style in the Operas of Benjamin Britten." (Music Education)

640. *Wilkey, Jay, "The Vocal Music of Alban Berg." (Music Education)

Iowa

641. Friedewald, Russell Edward, "A Formal and Stylistic Analysis of the Published Music of Samuel Barber." ix, 387 pp. (Ph.D., Theory, 1957)
UM 23,735. DA XVII.12, 3037.

Mich

642. *Henderson, Donald Gene, "The Music of Hans Pfitzner."

643. *Kushner, David Zakeri, "Ernest Bloch and His Symphonic Works."

Mich St

644. *Simpson, Ralph R., "William Grant Still: The Man and His Music." (Music Education)

645. *Wilson, Dean C., "A Formal and Stylistic Analysis of the Six Symphonies of Carl Nielsen." (Theory)

N Tex

646. Headley, Herrold Eugene, "The Choral Works of Arthur Honegger." xii, 285 pp. (Ph.D., Musicology, 1959) LC No.: Mic 59-1372. DA XIX.11, 2968.

647. McKenzie, Wallace Chessley, Jr., "The Music of Anton Webern." xiii, 494 pp. (Ph.D., Musicology, 1960) LC No.: Mic 60-2792. DA XXI.3, 640.

648. Trickey, Samuel Miller, "*Les Six.*" xiii, 330 pp. (Ph.D., Musicology, 1955) UM 14,373. DA XV.12, 2542.

N Wes

649. Gross, Bethuel S., "Modern Organ Literature." 159, vi pp. (Ph.D., Music, 1941)

650. Hart, Ralph Eugene, "Compositional Techniques in Choral Works of Stravinsky, Hindemith, Honegger, and Britten." vii, 316 pp. (Ph.D., Music, 1952)

651. Howden, Bruce Edward, "The Instrumental Theme and Variations: Its Treatment and Use by Twentieth-Century Composers." v, 203 pp. (Ph.D., Music, 1950)

652. Igou, Orin Lincoln, "Contemporary Symphonic Activity in Mexico with Special Regard to Carlos Chavez and Silvestre Revueltas." 593 pp. (Ph.D., Music, 1946)

653. Johns, Donald Charles, "Johann Nepomuk David's *Choralwerk:* A Study in the Evolution of a Contemporary Liturgical Organ Style." 295 pp. (Ph.D., Theory, 1960)

654. Krone, Max Thomas, "The Choral Works of Gustav Holst." 575 pp. (Ph.D., Music, 1940)

655. Larson, Robert Merl, "Stylistic Characteristics in *a cappella* Composition in the United States, 1940-1953, as Indicated by the Works of Jean Berger, David Diamond, Darius Milhaud, and Miklos Rozsa." 288 pp. (Ph.D., Music, 1953) UM 7047. DA XIV.2, 371.

656. Ramaley, John DeGraw, "The One-Movement Sonata-Form: Its Structural Treatment in Recent Instrumental Works." 186, ii pp. (Ph.D., Music, 1948)

657. Schmoll, Joseph Benjamin, "An Analytical Study of the Principal Instrumental Compositions of Wallingford Riegger." 348 pp. (Ph.D., Music, 1954) UM 10,318. DA XV.1, 130.

658. Taylor, Vernon H., "Contrapuntal Techniques in the Music of Béla Bartók." 318 pp. (Ph.D., Music, 1950)

659. Wathen, Lawrence Samuel, "Dissonance Treatment in the Instrumental Music of Samuel Barber." 147 pp. (Ph.D., Theory, 1960)

660. *Miller, James Allan, "The Music of Maurice Ravel as a Major Influence on the Music of Selected Twentieth-Century Composers." (Music Education)

NY Gr

661. Perle, George, "Serial Composition and Atonality." 211 pp. (Ph.D., Music, 1956)
    LC No.: Mic 59-1073. DA XIX.12, 3322.

662. *Friedheim, Philip, "The Problem of Structure in the Atonal Music of Arnold Schoenberg Prior to the Formulation of the Twelve-Tone System."

NY Ed

663. Hansler, George E., "Stylistic Characteristics and Trends in Contemporary British Choral Music." 731 pp. (Ph.D., Music Education, 1957)
    LC No.: Mic 58-651. DA XVIII.4, 1454.

664. Landau, Victor, "The Harmonic Theories of Paul Hindemith in Relation to His Practice as a Composer of Chamber Music." 342 pp. (Ph.D., Music Education, 1957)
    LC No.: Mic 58-664. DA XVIII.3, 1062.

665. McNaughton, Charles David, "Albert Stoessel, American Musician." 452 pp. in 2 vols. (Ph.D., Music Education, 1957)
    LC No.: Mic 58-654. DA XVIII.3, 1063.

666. Smith, Julia Frances, "Aaron Copland, His Work and Contribution to American Music." 648 pp. (Ph.D., Higher Education, 1952)
    UM 4534. DA XIII.1, 103.
    Published under the same title. New York, Dutton, 1955. 336 pp.

667. Suchoff, Benjamin, "Béla Bartók and a Guide to the *Mikrokosmos*." 389 pp. in 2 vols. (Ed.D., Music Education, 1956)
    UM 17,678. DA XVII.4, 867.

Peab

668. Brookhart, Charles E., "The Choral Music of Aaron Copland, Roy Harris, and Randall Thompson." iv, 293 pp. (Ph.D., Music, 1960)

669. Minsky, Henri S., *Ernest Bloch and His Music*. iv, 227 pp. (Ph.D., Music, 1945)
Peabody Contribution to Education No. 371.

Penn

670. Colucci, Matthew, "A Comparative Study of Contemporary Musical Theories in Selected Writings of Piston, Krenek, and Hindemith." 182 pp. (Ph.D., Theory, 1957)
UM 23,583. DA XVII.11, 2628.

Rad

671. Godoy, Susan, "Mexican Music from 1920 to 1953." 3 vols.: Vol. I, 463 pp., text; Vols. II and III, 707 pp., musical supplement. (Ph.D., Music, 1961)

672. Henning, Roslyn B., "The Use of Contrapuntal Techniques by Contemporary Composers." 890 pp. in 2 vols. (Ph.D., Music, 1947)

Roch

673. Colvin, Otis Herbert, "Charles Martin Loeffler: His Life and Works." 230 pp. in 2 vols. (Ph.D., Theory, 1959)

674. Halliday, John R., "Paul Hindemith—the Theorist." 420 pp. in 2 vols. (Ph.D., Theory, 1941)

675. Kirk, Edgar L., "Toward American Music: A Study of the Life and Music of Arthur George Farwell." 331 pp. in 2 vols. (Ph.D., Theory, 1959)

676. Lewis, Ralph B., "The Life and Music of Daniel Gregory Mason." 161 pp. (Ph.D., Theory, 1959)

677. Loucks, Richard N., "Arthur Shepherd." 1199 pp., text; 230 pp., examples; 100 ft. of microfilm—virtually all of Shepherd's music. (Ph.D., Theory, 1960)

678. McKeon, *Sister* Mary de LaSalle, "Stylistic Tendencies in Mid-Twentieth-Century American Piano Music." 310 pp. (Ph.D., Theory, 1957)

679. Moore, *Sister* Eleanor Marie, "A Study of the Vocal Works of Sir Edward Elgar." 388 pp. (Ph.D., Theory, 1961)

680. Pierson, Thomas C., "The Life and Music of John Alden Carpenter." 215 pp. (Ph.D., Theory, 1952)
UR 2295.

681. Rosner, *Sister* Mary Christian, "Contemporary Trends in the Musical Settings of the Liturgical Mass." 309 pp. (Ph.D., Theory, 1957)
UR 645.

682. Silliman, Cutler, "A Study of Musical Practices in Selected American String Quartets, 1930-1950." 215 pp. (Ph.D., Theory, 1954)
683. *Appledorn, Mary Jeanne van, "Stylistic Study of Debussy's *Pelléas et Mélisande*." (Theory)
684. *Bein, Joseph, "Harmonic Analysis of Debussy's *Images* for Orchestra." (Theory)
685. *Cole, Gerald, "Formal Organizations in the Contemporary Symphony." (Theory)
686. *Egner, Richard John, "The Metamorphosis of Traditional Cadence Concept Exemplified in the Music of Contemporary Soviet Composers." (Theory)
687. *Eide, Katherine M., "A Study of the Music of Charles Ives." (Theory)
688. *Moon, Charles, "An Analysis of Bartók's Third, Fourth, Fifth, and Sixth Quartets." (Theory)
689. *Moore, Robert Lee, "A Theoretical and Historical Analysis of Selected Hymn-Tunes Published since 1900." (Theory)
690. *Shumway, Stanley, "A Study of Instrumental Fugues by Contemporary American Composers." (Theory)
691. *Wigent, John, "Four Composers of the Northwestern University Group: Lutkin, Borowski, Oldberg, Noelte." (Theory)

S Cal

692. Dale, William Henry, "A Study of the Musico-Psychological Dramas of Vladimir Ivanovitch Rebikov." vii, 611 pp. (Ph.D., Musicology, 1955)
    UR 802.

Tex

693. *Broekema, Andrew, "A Stylistic Comparison of the Solo Vocal Works of Arnold Schoenberg, Alban Berg, and Anton Webern."
694. *Klein, Ursula, "The Stage Works of Rudolf Wagner-Régeny."
695. *Swanay, John, "The Rise, Growth, and Diffusion of Dodecaphonic Techniques."

Wash

696. Christensen, Louis, "The Orchestral Works of Gösta Nystroem: A Critical Study." 259 pp. (Ph.D., Music, 1961)
697. *Krebs, Stanley Dale, "Soviet Music: 1920-1950."
698. *Skinner, Wilfred J., "Dissonance Practices in Music of the 1920s."

Wash StL

699. *Kremer, Rudolf, "The Organ Sonata in the Twentieth Century."
700. *Stellhorn, Martin, "The Chorale-Prelude Principle in the Twentieth Century."

W Res

701. Newman, William S., "The Present Trend of the Sonata Idea." 172 pp. (Ph.D., Music, 1939)
702. *Walters, William R., "Twentieth-Century Trends in Church Music."

ETHNOMUSICOLOGICAL AND
NATIONAL SUBJECTS

Cal LA

703. Malm, William, "Japanese *Nagauta* Music." 2 vols.: Vol. I, 372 pp., text; Vol. II, 103 pp., transcriptions. (Ph.D., Music, 1959)

704. May, Elizabeth, "Japanese Children's Music before and after Contact with the West." 205 pp. (Ph.D., Music, 1958)

705. *Brown, Robert E., "The *Tāla* (Rhythm) System of South Indian Classical Music."

706. *Farhat, Hormoz, "Rhythm and Melody in Persian Music."

Cath

707. Wells, L. Jeanette, *A History of the Music Festival at Chautauqua Institution from 1874 to 1957*. Washington, D. C., The Catholic University of America Press, 1958. x, 310 pp. (Ph.D., Musicology, 1958)

Cor

708. Gizzarelli, Ermanno Francis, "An Historical Survey of Italian Folk Song and a Critical Estimate of Modern Research." 185 pp. (Ph.D., Musicology, 1938)
    Abstract in *Abstracts of Theses* (Cornell University, 1938)

Flor

709. Der Hovhanissian, Harpik, "Armenian Music: A Cosmopolitan Art." 292 pp. in 2 vols. (Ed.D., Music Education, 1956)
    UM 17,024. DA XVI.12, 2475.

Harv

710. LaRue, Adrian Jan, "The Okinawan Classical Songs: An Analytical and Comparative Study." 260 pp., 16 plates. (Ph.D., Music, 1952)

711. *England, Nicholas M., "Music in the Societies of Certain Groups of Bushmen in South Africa."

Ill

712. Wolf, Edward C., "Lutheran Church Music in America during the Eighteenth and Early Nineteenth Centuries." 454 pp. (Ph.D., Musicology, 1960)

713. *Hill, Double E., "A Study of Taste in American Church Music as Reflected in the Music of the Methodist Episcopal Church to 1900."

Ind

714. Mahmoud, Parviz, "A Theory of Persian Music and Its Relation to Western Practice." 164 pp. (Ph.D., Theory, 1957) UM 19,468. DA XVII.5, 1091.

715. McCorkle, Donald Macomber, "Moravian Music in Salem: A German-American Heritage." 431 pp. (Ph.D., Musicology, 1958)
    LC No.: Mic 59-333. DA XX.2, 688.

716. Nettl, Bruno, "American Indian Music North of Mexico: Its Styles and Areas." 254 pp. (Ph.D., Musicology, 1953) UM 5873. DA XIII.5, 834.
    Published as *North American Indian Musical Styles.* Philadelphia, The American Folklore Society, 1954. *Memoirs of the American Folklore Society, XLV.* ix, 51 pp.

717. Yerbury, Grace Helen, "Styles and Schools of the Art-Song in America, 1720-1850." 441 pp. (Ph.D., Theory, 1953) UM 6459. DA XIII.6, 1219.

718. *Bryant, Melville C., Jr., "Derivation and Development of the American Negro Gospel Songs." (Music Education)

Iowa

719. Kent, Ralph McVety, "A Study of Oratorios and Sacred Cantatas Composed in America before 1900." 2 vols.: Vol. I, x, 319 pp.; Vol. II, 281 pp., including photographic reproductions of about 400 examples from printed scores and manuscripts. (Ph.D., Music, 1954) UM 9583. DA XIV.10, 1757.

720. Phelps, Roger Paul, "The History and Practice of Chamber Music in the United States from Earliest Times up to 1875." 2 vols.: Vol. I, xx, 547 pp., text; Vol. II, 408 pp., appendices and musical examples. (Ph.D., Music Education, 1951) UR 2267.

Mich

721. Britton, Allen P., "Theoretical Introductions in American Tune-Books to 1800." 697 pp. (Ph.D., Musicology, 1950) UM 1505. DA X.1, 97.

Minn

722. *Canon, Cornelius B., "The Federal Music Project of the Works Progress Administration."

723. *Cartford, Gerhard M., "A Study of Music among Norwegian Immigrants to the United States from 1825 to 1925."

N Car

724. Garrett, Allen, "The Works of William Billings." 177 pp. (Ph.D., Music, 1952)

N Wes

725. Gould, Cassius Wallace, "An Analysis of the Folk Music in the Oaxaca and Chiapas Areas of Mexico." 327 pp. (Ph.D., Music, 1954)
    UM 9237. DA XIV.11, 2085.
726. Hohmann, Rupert Karl, "The Church Music of the Old Order Amish of the United States." 262 pp. (Ph.D., Music History and Literature, 1959)
    LC No.: Mic 60-436. DA XX.9, 3769.
727. Pernecky, John Martin, "A Musico-Ethnological Approach to the Instrumental Music of Béla Bartók." 184 pp. (Ph.D., Music Education, 1956)
    UM 19,585. DA XVI.12, 2476.
728. Purdy, William Earl, "Music in Mormon Culture, 1830-1876." 383 pp. (Ph.D., Music History and Literature, 1960)

NY Gr

729. Brandel, Rose, "The Music of Central Africa." 2 vols.: Vol. I, 231 pp., text; Vol. II, 139 pp., transcriptions. (Ph.D., Music, 1959)

NY Ed

730. Kuh, Koh-nie, "A Musicological Study of the Important Tonal Systems of the T'ang Dynasty (A.D. 618-907)." 271 pp. (Ed.D., Music Education, 1942)
731. *Armour, Eugene, "The Melodic and Rhythmic Characteristics of the Music of the Traditional Ballad Variants Found in the Southern Appalachians."

Peab

732. Wiant, Bliss Mitchell, *The Character and Function of Music in Chinese Culture*. viii, 325 pp. (Ph.D., Musicology, 1946)
    Peabody Contribution to Education No. 376.
733. *Hall, Harry H., "The Evolution of the Moravian Wind Ensemble in America: A Chapter in the History of the American Wind Band."

734. *Thompson, James William, "Music and Musical Activities in New England, 1800-1838."

Penn

735. Gerson, Robert Aaron, *Music in Philadelphia.* Philadelphia, Theo. Presser Co., 1940. 422 pp. (Ph.D., Music, 1939)

Prin

736. Powers, Harry Stone, "The Background of the South Indian *Rāga*-System." 3 vols. in 2: Vol. I, xv, 222 pp., text and bibliography; Vol. II, 84, iii pp., text, 10 pp., music. (Ph.D., Music, 1959)
LC No.: Mic 60-2106. DA XXI.1, 206.

Rad

737. Pian, (Mrs.) Rulan Chao, "Sources of Music in the Sung Dynasty: 960-1279 A.D." 306 pp. (Ph.D., Music, 1960)
(Degree program carried on jointly with the Department of Music and the Department of Far Eastern Languages, Harvard University)

Roch

738. Horn, Dorothy, "A Study of the Folk Hymns of Southeastern America." 133 pp. (Ph.D., Theory, 1952)
739. Howell, Gordon P., "The Development of Music in Canada." 544 pp. (Ph.D., Theory, 1959)
740. LeMon, Melvin William, "Pennsylvania Anthracite Miners' Folksongs." 2 vols.: Vol. I, 93 pp. and 5 pp., commentary; Vol. II, 107 pp., music; 15 phonograph records. (Ph.D., Musicology, 1941)

S Cal

741. Dean, Talmage Whitman, "The Organ in Eighteenth-Century English Colonial America." 276 pp. (Ph.D., Musicology, 1960)
LC No.: Mic 60-5474. DA XXI.6, 1583.
742. Engelke, Hans, "A Study of Ornaments in American Tune-Books, 1760-1800." 217 pp. (Ph.D., Musicology, 1960)
LC No.: Mic 60-558. DA XX.10, 4130.
743. Hirt, Charles C., "Graeco-Slavonic Chant Traditions Evident in the Part-Writing of the Russian Orthodox Church." 461 pp. (Ph.D., Music, 1946)
744. Reece, Donald Cortez, "A Study of Selected Folksongs, Col-

lected Mainly in West Virginia." 1083 pp. (Ph.D., Musicol ogy, 1955)

745. Smith, Carlton York, "Lutheran Hymnody in the United States before 1850." xx, 302 pp. (Ph.D., Musicology, 1956)

746. Smith, Wilbur, "A Study of the Use of the English Folk-Music Scales in Eleven Selected Symphonies." xiii, 285 pp. (Ph.D., Musicology, 1956)

747. Wilcox, Glenn, "Jacob Kimball, Jr. (1761-1826): His Life and Works." xii, 263 pp. (Ph.D., Musicology, 1957)
    UR 3058.

748. Wilkes, William, "Borrowed Music in Mormon Hymnals." viii, 316 pp. (Ph.D., Musicology, 1957)

749. Willhide, J. Lawrence, "Samuel Holyoke, American Music-Educator." xiii, 421 pp. (Ph.D., Musicology, 1954)
    UR 3068.

U Theol

750. Allwardt, Anton Paul, "Sacred Music in New York, 1800-1850." 394 pp. (D.S.M., 1950)

751. Hjortsvang, Carl T., "Scandinavian Contributions to American Sacred Music." 255 pp. (D.S.M., 1951)

752. Olson, Lee O. G., "A History of Swedish Church Music." 173 pp. (D.S.M., 1946)

753. Sims, John Norman, "The Hymnody of the Camp-Meeting Tradition." 181 pp. (D.S.M., 1960)

754. *Espina, Noni, "Music in the Philippine Islands."

755. *Heaton, Charles Huddleston, "The Disciples of Christ and Sacred Music."

756. *McCormick, David W., "Oliver Holden, Composer and Anthologist."

W Res

757. Cook, Harold, "Shaker Music: A Manifestation of American Folk Culture." 301 pp. (Ph.D., Music, 1947)

INSTRUMENTS

Cal LA

758. Chapman, Roger E., "The Books on Instruments in the *Harmonie Universelle* of Marin Mersenne." 1170 pp. in 3 vols. (Ph.D., Music, 1954)

Published as *Marin Mersenne: Harmonie Universelle. The Books on Instruments.* Translated by Roger E. Chapman. The Hague, Martinus Nijhoff, 1957. xii, 596 pp.

Cath

759. Stauffer, Donald W., *Intonation Deficiencies of Wind Instruments.* Washington, D. C., The Catholic University of America Press, 1954. xiv, 191 pp. (Ph.D., Musicology, 1954)

Flor

760. *Kinney, Gordon J., "A Stylistic Analysis of the Musical Literature for the Unaccompanied Violoncello." (Theory)

Harv

761. Coerne, Louis Adolphe, "The Evolution of Modern Orchestration." 438 pp. (Ph.D., Music, 1905)

Published under the same title. New York, The Macmillan Co., 1908. 280 pp.

762. Shackford, Charles Reeves, "Intonation in Ensemble String Performance: An Objective Study." 269 pp. (Ph.D., Music, 1954)

763. Titcomb, Caldwell, "The Kettledrums in Western Europe: Their History outside the Orchestra." 2 vols.: 575 pp., including plates; portfolio containing large illustration. (Ph.D., Music, 1952)

Iowa

764. Hedlund, Harry Jean, "A Study of Certain Representative Compositions for Woodwind Ensembles, *ca.* 1695-1815." 223 pp. (Ph.D., Music Education, 1959)

LC No.: Mic 59-1683. DA XIX.12, 3321.

765. Starkey, Willard A., "The History and Practice of Ensemble Music for Lip-Reed Instruments." x, 599 pp. (Ph.D., Music Education, 1954)

UM 10,246. DA XV.1, 131.

766. *Titus, Robert A., "The Solo Music for the Clarinet in the Eighteenth Century." (Music)

Mich

767. Riley, Maurice Winton, "The Teaching of Bowed Instruments from 1511 to 1756." 466 pp. (Ph.D., Musicology, 1954) UM 8236. DA XIV.7, 1089.
768. Russell, Myron Edward, "The Oboe: A Comparison Study of Specifications with Musical Effectiveness." 321 pp. (Ph.D., Musicology, 1953) UM 5723. DA XIII.5, 835.

Minn

769. Mayer, Francis N., "A History of Scoring for Band." (Ph.D., Musicology, 1957)

N Car

770. Gates, Willis C., "The Literature for Unaccompanied Solo Violin." v, 347 pp. (Ph.D., Music, 1950)
771. *Klitz, Brian Kent, "Solo Sonatas and Duos for Bassoon before 1750."

N Wes

772. Malek, Vincent F., "A Study of Embouchure and Trumpet-Cornet Mouthpiece Measurements." 184 pp. (Ph.D., Music, 1953) UM 6219. DA XIII.6, 1217.
773. Schmidt, Lloyd John, "A Practical and Historical Source-Book for the Recorder." 641 pp. (Ph.D., Music Education, 1959) LC No.: Mic 59-4837. DA XX.6, 2325.
774. *Gangware, Edgar Brand, "Percussion Instruments: Their History and Use in Orchestration." (Theory)

NY Gr

775. *Antos, Kalman, "The German Organ in the Sixteenth Century."

Roch

776. Husted, Benjamin, "The Brass Ensemble: Its History and Music." ix, 445 pp. in 2 vols. (Ph.D., Theory, 1955)
777. *Bunjes, Paul George, "Theories regarding Tonal Structures of the Organ as Developed by Schlick, Praetorius, and Werckmeister." (Theory)

PHILOSOPHY
(including Aesthetics)

Bos

778. *Croan, Robert J., "Changing Concepts of the Perfect Opera: A History of Operatic Aesthetics."

Chi

779. Cowan, Denis, "Morphology and Value in Music." 185 pp. (Ph.D., Music, 1960)

Colum

780. Lippman, Edward Arthur, "Music and Space: A Study in the Philosophy of Music." 419 pp. (Ph.D., Musicology, 1952) UM 4211. DA XII.5, 631.

Harv

781. Elston, Arnold, "On Musical Dynamics." 167 pp. (Ph.D., Music, 1939)
    Summary in *Summaries of Theses . . . 1939* (Harvard University, 1942), pp. 283-286.
782. Irvine, Demar Buel, "The Expression of Ideas and Emotions in Music: A Contribution to the Practical Esthetics of Musical Composition." 257 pp. (Ph.D., Music, 1937)
    Summary in *Summaries of Theses . . . 1937* (Harvard University, 1938), pp. 316-317.

Ind

783. Darack, Arthur, "Aesthetics of Music: Early Greek Views." 181 pp. (Ph.D., Theory, 1951)
    UM 10,420. DA XIV.12, 2363.
784. Youngblood, Joseph E., "Music and Language: Some Related Analytical Techniques." 127 pp. (Ph.D., Theory, 1960)

Iowa

785. Blum, Fred, "Susanne Langer's Music Aesthetics." xxv, 435 pp. (Ph.D., Musicology, 1959)
    LC No.: Mic 59-3786. DA XX.3, 1037.
786. Merchant, (Mrs.) Gloria Bader, "A Translation and Critique of *La Musique et la vie intérieure* by Lucien Bourguès and Alexandre Denéréaz (A Psycho-Musico-Aesthetic Study)."

Part I, 157 pp., commentary; Part II, 796 pp., translation; Part III, 177 pp., music examples and tables. (Ph.D., Musicology, 1961)

787. *Schroder, Charles Frederick, "The Aesthetic Bases of Musical Truth and Realism in the Nineteenth Century."

N Car

788. Muns, George Ehrman, Jr., "Climax in Music." 491 pp. (Ph.D., Music, 1955)

N Wes

789. Martini, Clare Joseph, "Maritain and Music." 214 pp. (Ph.D., Music, 1958)
    LC No.: Mic 58-5769. DA XIX.7, 1781.

NY Ed

790. Singleton, Ira C., "The Rationality of Eighteenth-Century Musical Classicism." 412 pp. in 2 vols. (Ph.D., Music Education, 1954)

791. Wiedman, Robert W., "Expressionism in Music." 380 pp. in 2 vols. (Ph.D., Music Education, 1955)

Penn

792. Michell, Joyce, *Symbolism in Music and Poetry*. Philadelphia, 1944. 54 pp. (Ph.D., Musicology, 1944)

Wisc

793. Pautz, Zane Ernest W., "An Historical and Analytical Study of Mysticism in Music." 112 pp. (Ph.D., Music, 1957)
    UM 24,316. DA XVII.11, 2631.

Yale

794. Sadowsky, (Mrs.) Rosalie D. Landres, "Jean-Baptiste *Abbé* Du-Bos: The Influence of Cartesian and Neo-Aristotelian Ideas on Music Theory and Practice." 278, xii pp. (Ph.D., History of Music, 1960)

THEORY

Cal LA

795. Edwards, Arthur C., "A Theory of Melody." 374 pp. (Ph.D., Music, 1954)
    Published as *The Art of Melody*. New York, Philosophical Library, 1956. xxx, 266 pp.

796. Wienpahl, Robert W., "The Emergence of Tonality." 447 pp. (Ph.D., Music, 1953)

Cath

797. *Mackey, *Sister* Mary Lourdes, "The Evolution of the Leading-Tone in Western European Music."

Colum

798. Mann, Alfred, "The Theory of Fugue." 467 pp. (Ph.D., Musicology, 1955)
    UM 12,452. DA XV.8, 1412.
    Published as *The Study of Fugue*. New Brunswick, New Jersey, Rutgers University Press, 1958, viii, 341 pp.

Cor

799. Smither, Howard Elbert, "Theories of Rhythm in the Nineteenth and Twentieth Centuries, with a Contribution to the Theory of Rhythm for the Study of Twentieth-Century Music." 450 pp. (Ph.D., Musicology, 1960)
    LC No.: Mic 61-18. DA XXI.8, 2319.

Flor

800. *Patterson, Andy James, "Principles of Musical Analysis: A Survey of the Principal Concepts of Analysis, with an Anthology of Illustrative Examples." (Music Theory)

Harv

801. Cazden, Norman, "Musical Consonance and Dissonance." 978 pp. in 2 vols. (Ph.D., Music, 1948)

Ind

802. Gustin, (Mrs.) Molly, "A Theory of Tonality." 164 pp. (Ph.D., Theory, 1961)

803. Haggh, Raymond, "Hugo Riemann's *Geschichte der Musiktheorie im IX-XIX. Jahrhundert*, Books I and II: A Translation

with Commentary and Annotated Bibliography." 2 vols.: Vol. I, 487 pp., translation; Vol. II, 154 pp., commentary and bibliography. (Ph.D., Theory, 1961)

804. Jorgenson, Dale A., "A History of Theories of the Minor Triad." 169 pp. (Ph.D., Theory, 1957)
UM 22,691. DA XVII.10, 2281.

805. Lamm, Robert Carson, "The Evolution of the Secondary Dominant Concept." 261 pp. (Ph.D., Theory, 1954)
UM 10,150. DA XIV.11, 2087.

806. Thomson, William Ennis, "A Clarification of the Tonality Concept." 244 pp. (Ph.D., Theory, 1952)
UM 4380. DA XII.6, 800.

807. *Burke, James Robert, "A History of the Theory of Non-Harmonic Tones." (Theory)

808. *Kliewer, Vernon L., "The Concept of Organic Unity in Music Criticism and Analysis." (Theory)

809. *Mandelbaum, Joel, "Nineteen-Tone Equal Temperament as a Potential Basis for Musical Composition." (Theory)

810. *Nagosky, John, "Thresholds of Sinusoid Mixtures." (Theory)

Iowa

811. Krueger, Theodore Howard, "*Der freie Satz* by Heinrich Schenker: A Complete Translation and Re-editing." 2 vols.: Vol. I, lxxvii, 378 pp., commentary and translation; Vol. II, viii, 60 pp., supplement of musical examples. (Ph.D., Theory, 1960)

812. Mann, Chester D., Jr., "A Theory of the Aural Interpretation of Tonal Combinations." x, 220 pp. (Ph.D., Musicology and Theory, 1952)
UR 1908.

813. Service, Alfred Roy, Jr., "A Study of the Cadence as a Factor in Musical Intelligibility in Selected Piano Sonatas by American Composers." 347 pp. (Ph.D., Musicology, 1958)
LC No.: Mic 58-5859. DA XIX.7, 1781.

N Car

814. Alden, Edgar H., "The Role of the Motive in Musical Structure." 201 pp. (Ph.D., Musicology, 1956)

N Tex

815. Dorn, Gerhardt George, "Harmonic Mutation as a Function of Stimulus Intensity." 131 pp. (Ph.D., Theory, 1955)
UM 14,370. DA XV.12, 2540.

Ohio

816. Poland, Bernard William, "An Investigation of Some Aural and Notational Elements in Music Theory." vii, 127 pp. (Ph.D., Music, 1960)
LC No.: Mic 60-2129. DA XXI.1, 205.

Roch

817. Alette, Carl, "Theories of Rhythm." 323 pp. in 2 vols. (Ph.D., Theory, 1951)
UR 42.
818. Benward, Bruce Charles, "A Proposal for the Analysis of Motion Factors in Music." 269 pp. (Ph.D., Theory, 1951)
819. Braman, Wallis, "The Use of Silence in the Instrumental Works of Representative Composers: Baroque, Classic, Romantic." 337 pp. (Ph.D., Theory, 1956)
820. Kauko, Väinö Olavi, "The Development of a Phenomenological Approach to Music as Seen in Selected Theories of Tonal Organization." 219 pp. (Ph.D., Theory, 1959)
821. Sherburn, Merrell L., "An Investigation and Classification of Non-Functional Harmonic Movement." 605 pp. (Ph.D., Theory, 1959)
822. Webb, John, "Compositional Features of Original Music for One Piano, Four Hands." 223 pp. in 2 vols. (Ph.D., Theory, 1959)
823. *Shatzkin, Merton, "The Evolution of Superimposed Harmonic Entities." (Theory)

W Res

824. Evans, Edward G., Jr., "An Investigation of Harmonic Tension." (Ph.D., Music, 1951)
825. Goodwin, Gladys Foulke, "The Harmonic Cross-Relation: Its History and Analysis." 127 pp. (Ph.D., Music, 1937)
826. Schaeffer, Myron S., "Harmonic Analysis and Musical Style: Harmonic Causal Factors of Style Recognition in Music; Methods of Analysis." 201 pp. (Ph.D., Music, 1937)

MISCELLANEOUS

Colum

827. Loft, Abram, "Musicians' Guild and Union: A Consideration of the Evolution of Protective Organization among Musicians." 408 pp. (Ph.D., Musicology, 1950)
UM 1870. DA X.4, 321.

N Wes

828. Holsinger, Clyde William, "A History of Choral Conducting with Emphasis on the Time-Beating Techniques Used in the Successive Historical Periods." 357 pp. (Ph.D., Music, 1954)
UM 10,301. DA XIV.12, 2363.

U Theol

829. Simmons, Morgan, "Latin Hymnody: Its Resurgence in English Usage." (D.S.M., 1961)

Including 402# or released.

Net : 427

INDEX OF AUTHORS

= Small dissertation
(not all on complete)

INDEX OF SUBJECTS

(The numbers appearing here are those assigned the dissertations for the Third Edition)

Frye, Walter, 248
fugas, 76
fugue: 531, 690; before Bach, 423; Bach, 269, 408; theory of, 798

Gabrieli, Andrea, 256
Gabrieli, Giovanni, 134
Gafurius, Franchinus, 232
Gagliano, Marco da, 384
Galuppi, Baldassare, 521
Gamble, John, 266
Gassmann, Florian, 527
Gastoldi, G. G., 204
Gaveaux, Pierre, 524
Geminiani, Francesco, 350
Genet, Elzéar, 139
Gershwin, George, 613
Gesualdo, Carlo, 175
Gibbons, Christopher, 336
Gibbons, Orlando, 218
Glarean, Henry, 1, 136
Goethe, J. W. von, 539, 569, 570
Goetschius, Percy, 585
Gothic music, 9
Gottschalk, L. M., 579
Goudimel, Claude, 172
Greece, aesthetics in ancient, 783
Gregory, William, the Younger, 425
Grétry, A. E. M., 512
Griffes, C. T., 619, 631
Guarini, G. B., 68
guitar, 573

Hadley, Henry, 621
Hammerschmidt, Andreas, 421, 462
Handel, G. F., 264, 276, 279, 286, 293, 300, 327, 333, 456
Handl, Jacob, 145
harmony, harmonic: analysis, 826; Beethoven's modulation techniques, 594; of A. Berg, 627; cadence, 686, 813; chordal concept, 8; in classical form, 467; contemporary, 625; cross-relation, 825; h. of Debussy, 626, 684; evolution of h. consciousness, 31; evolution of the leading-tone, 797; h. in the English fancy, 435; in 14th-c. France, 32; of the French Six, 606; h. style of Lasso, 205; in madrigals of Gesualdo, 175; minor triad, 804; Mozart's h. lan-

guage, 530; h. mutation, 815; non-functional h. movement, 821; non-h. tones, 807; of Palestrina, 85; h. patterns, 532; from Rameau to 1900, 303; early Renaissance h., 118; h. rhythm, 499, 565, 623; secondary dominant, 805; superimposed h. 823; supertonic 7th, 428; h. tension, 824; h. theories of Hindemith, 664
harpsichord music, 440, 488; see also: concerto, duet, keyboard, sonata, suite
Harris, Roy, 668
Hassler, Hans Leo, 51, 212
Haydn, F. J., 469, 473, 500, 508
Haydn, Michael, 514, 538
Heinichen, J. D., 402
Hindemith, Paul, 650, 664, 670, 674
Hingeston, John, 340
Hoffmann, E. T. A., 598
Holden, Oliver, 756
Holst, Gustav, 654
Holyoke, Samuel, 749
Honegger, Arthur, 637, 646, 650
Horn, Charles Edward, 557
Hüllmandel, N.-J., 502
Humfrey, Pelham, 368
Hummel, J. N., 576
Huygens, Christian, 451
hymns, hymnody: 159; American tune-books, 721; in the works of J. S. Bach, 273; of the camp-meeting tradition, 753; English, 48; folk-h. in America, 738; Italian organ-h., 91; Latin, 829; Lutheran, 745; Mormon, 748; Mozarabic, 34; ornaments in American tune-books, 742; by Porta, 152; by Prudentius, 34; Roman Catholic, 30; tunes, 689

illumination in music MSS, 200
Impressionism, 631, 632
India: the *Rāga* system, 736; the *Tāla* system, 705
Indian music, American, 716
Indy, Vincent d', 587, 591
In Nomine, 226
intonation, 759, 762
Isaac, Heinrich, 122, 207
Ives, Charles, 687
Ivrea, Codex, motets of, 14

112